Dollars and Sense

Ten Fundamentals of Financial Success

By David Philipp Greene

Dollars and Sense: Ten Fundamentals of Financial Success
Copyright © 2012 by David Philipp Greene.

All rights reserved. No part of this book may be reproduced or transmitted in any form or by any means without written permission of the author.

Books are available for special promotions and premiums. For details, contact Special Markets, LINX, Corp., Box 613, Great Falls, VA 22066, or e-mail special-markets@linxcorp.com.

Published by LINX.
LINX, Corp.
Box 613
Great Falls, VA 22066
www.linxcorp.com

Edited by Ali Ferguson
Book Design by Paul Fitzgerald
Illustrations by Michael Halbert

Printed in the United States of America.

No one approach fits all investors. Please consult an experienced investment professional who understands your financial circumstances, your goals, and your ability to assume risk before adopting this or any other investment approach. No product recommendations are made by or should be inferred from this book.

This book is based in part on some of my own hard work and ideas. This book is based in larger part, however, on the hard work and ideas of many people who came before me.

In particular, I have relied extensively on the research and training provided to me by the investment professionals, analysts, and others at Bernstein Global Wealth Management, a unit of AllianceBernstein L.P. ("Bernstein"). Although Bernstein has neither sponsored this book, nor expressed any opinion about its content, the subject matter is influenced by Bernstein's research and the training I received there. Investment advice should be uniquely tailored to each reader's individual circumstances, however, and should not be based on this book alone. Please contact the author if you would like additional information.

For Gayle,
and for
Robert, James, and Elizabeth.

Acknowledgments

I have been fortunate to work with many phenomenal people at Bernstein Global Wealth Management, including two extraordinarily talented managing directors, Evan Deoul and Mary Ann Best. Evan hired and inspired me; Mary Ann has taken every opportunity to support me even with crazy ideas like writing this book.

Haven Pell provided me with great mentorship and friendship at Bernstein. He taught me that it does not matter what I say; it matters only what people hear. He taught me that good advice is worthless unless it can be followed. Haven's advice informed the way I wrote this book, and his advice continues to inform the way I advise my clients to this day.

I am grateful to work alongside a number of colleagues and clients who have taught me valuable lessons about finance, family, fellowship, and faith.

A few years ago, I met an investor by the name of Marshall Wallach. Marshall wrote a short book—15 pages in length—titled *Marshall's 10 Rules for the Taxable Investor*, which became the catalyst for this project. In the brief time Marshall and I spent together, I came to admire many things about him—not the least of which was his ability to sum up in 15 pages what took me many more.

Several friends and professional partners read early drafts of this book, including Dan Adragna, Susan Butler, Lisa Cines, Mark Ellenbogen, Ken Falke, John Forster, Scott Frederick, Mike Frost, Michael Grace, Michelle Haley, Oksana Hoey, Eric Horvitz, Lauren Keenan, Lisa McCurdy, Gren Millard, Lew Saret, Michael Stoltzfus, Ed Weiss, Yvette Woods, and Terry Zerwick. Their advice and assistance was invaluable, and this book is better for their input. Any faults that remain are entirely my own.

Robert, James, and Elizabeth Greene—my three children— helped select the graphics that start each chapter of this book. They are my joy and my inspiration.

Finally, I'd like to thank my wife, Gayle. I wouldn't have completed this book—or much else over the past 15 years—if it were not for her support. While I hover over my keyboard, Gayle handles almost everything else in our family's life. Whether she is supervising the fire department as our house nearly burns to the ground or driving our children to the emergency room, Gayle perseveres with grace, love, and seemingly infinite patience. And I'm not joking about the fire department, by the way. Last year, as I was writing this book, Gayle knocked on the door to our bedroom office. "I'm not saying that you need to stop working," she said. "I just want you to know that I've called the fire department and am taking the children across the street until the firemen arrive."

For always reminding me—gently and patiently—what is most fundamental, I will always be grateful to Gayle.

Table of Contents

Foreword		
Fundamental #1:	Making Money	7
Fundamental #2:	Spending (and Saving) Money	19
Fundamental #3:	It Is Easier to Get There If You Know Where You Are Going	29
Fundamental #4:	What You Keep Is More Important Than What You Earn	39
Fundamental #5:	Diversify Your Investments	55
Fundamental #6	What You Buy Matters More Than Who Buys It for You	65
Fundamental #7:	You Are Already Off Course	81
Fundamental #8:	The Source of Information Matters	89
Fundamental #9:	Get Financial Advice from People Whose Financial Interests Are Aligned with Yours	95
Fundamental #10:	Evaluating Your Investment Manager	103
Epilogue		115
Words of Wisdom		121
Endnotes		127

Foreword

Four years of studying economics at Harvard—and another two studying at Harvard for an MBA—didn't adequately prepare me for the challenges of advising clients about their personal finances. A fundamental education in economic and business theory has been important to my understanding of how markets behave. An understanding of economic and business theory is necessary—but not sufficient—to guide investors as they navigate through the markets.

Most economic and business theory starts with the presupposition of fully rational investors. Rational investors are never gripped by greed or fear. They simply and perfectly evaluate the objective risks and rewards of various investment choices.

Although the idea of a rational investor is the cornerstone of basic economic theory, in practice, investors are never rational. All human beings are gripped by irrational fears and desires. At times, we are all inspired by unrealistic dreams and held back by imagined risks.

Over longer periods of time, the various irrational motivations of the millions of economic actors in our markets tend to balance out: markets do act rationally, good companies outperform ill-managed companies, and risks are rewarded in proportionate measure.

Over shorter periods of time, the irrational nature of markets and the emotions of investors can prove to be difficult challenges. My job as an investor and as a financial advisor is not to provide an academic description of how markets work. My job is to help real people respond to real markets in a way that preserves and builds wealth over time.

Without good advice to support them, investors too often react wrongly to market fluctuations, and they too often react at the wrong times. The cautionary tale of Icarus and Daedalus provides an illustration of the consequences of going to extremes:

The Fall of Icarus

Seeking to escape exile from the isle of Crete, Daedalus looked to the heavens as the only route open to him and his son, Icarus. So, Daedalus crafted two pairs of wings from feathers and wax.

Before taking flight, Daedalus warned his son: "Take care to fly halfway between the sun and the sea. If you fly too high, the sun's heat will melt the wax that binds your wings. If you fly too low, the sea's mist will dampen the feathers that give you lift. Instead, aim for the middle course and avoid the extremes."

However, Icarus was exhilarated by his newfound power of flight. He soared high into the heavens, ignoring his father's warning. Soon, the sun melted the wax that bonded his wings.

Icarus fell from the sky, followed by the gently wafting feathers that held him in flight, and he was swallowed by the swelling seas.

–Adapted from *Metamorphoses* by Ovid.

Sometimes, I imagine myself in the role of Daedalus: providing warnings and cautions as my clients journey through up and down markets.

The story of Icarus and Daedalus is thousands of years old. The moral of the Icarus and Daedalus story is still relevant to real-world investors today. We need to look back only over the last 20 years to see a modern retelling of the story of Icarus and Daedalus in financial terms.

From 1995 through 1999, the U.S. stock market enjoyed a remarkable run: $1 million invested in the S&P 500 at the start of 1995 would have soared to $3.5 million by the end of 1999. Excited by such spectacular growth, investors poured more than $350 billion into stock mutual funds in 2000—close to double what they had put in the year before.

Investors' fervors of greed were quickly overtaken by tremors of fear. From 2000 to 2002, the S&P plunged 38%. Investors went into full panic mode, bailing out of the stock market and transferring their depleted assets into cash or bonds. In 2003, the stock market rebounded dramatically and returned 29% for the year. The investors who retreated into cash missed out on this recovery.

Investors were greedy—flying too close to the sun—when they should have been fearful. They were fearful—flying too close to the sea—when they should have been greedy. Investors continually refused to take the middle course.

Our memories as investors are remarkably short. Just a few years after the dot-com bubble and bust, markets played out a similar story. Again, investors realized similarly poor results.

From 2003 until the end of 2007, stocks were up more than 60%. Investors poured money into the equity markets. From September 2008 through March 2009, stocks were down 40%, and investors fled the market in droves, thereby missing the nearly 100% rise in the market that followed in the next two years.

These stories of greed and fear are not limited to Greek mythology and the U.S. equity markets. Investors have acted no more rationally in other investment categories. Over the last 20 years, we have seen dramatic bubbles and busts in the housing market; commodities like gold, silver, and oil; stocks; bonds; and currencies. In each case, investors have bought high, sold low, and lost a lot of money in the process.

Even experts have difficulty spotting bubbles. One of the first and foremost books on bubbles in financial markets is Charles Mackay's 1841 treatise, *Extraordinary Popular Delusions and the Madness of Crowds*. Drawing from history, Mackay illustrated how easy—and how financially devastating—it is to get swept up in a market bubble.

Three years after Mackay published his book, a bubble in British railroad stocks emerged. Mackay, the leading expert on market bubbles of his day, urged investors to buy British railroad stocks late in 1845, writing in October of that year that "those who sound the alarm of an approaching railway crisis have somewhat exaggerated the danger." Mackay concluded, "there is no reason whatever to fear" a crash in the market.

Mackay couldn't have been more wrong. From 1845 to 1850, railroad stocks lost two-thirds of their value. The moral of this story: investors should always be careful to guard against the assertions of experts who say they can detect bubbles before they burst.[1]

Investing on the basis of a market's recent history—any market's recent history—is like trying to drive a car while looking in the rearview mirror. It isn't the road—or the investments—that cause the damage from the crash; it is the way we drive (or, in my world, the way we invest).

One thing is for certain: we cannot change the markets. However, we can change the way we *react* to the markets. As investors, we can better protect and build wealth by looking forward instead of backward.

Ultimately, the most important part of my job—the single most valuable service I provide—is to help clients act rationally in the face of an irrational world. Together, my clients and I plan for a successful future in the face of markets that are always unpredictable and often unpleasant.

As a financial advisor, I try to help abate the fear and greed that are a natural part of our psyche but can be so damaging to us as investors. In that way, I endeavor to protect and prudently manage the wealth that clients have entrusted to me.

Helping clients build and preserve wealth requires more than an understanding of academic finance and theoretical economics. Practical investing—the practice of investing—is more nuanced. The rewards of practicing practical investing are significant in both emotional and financial terms.

I consider it an honor and a privilege to join my clients on their journeys toward successful financial futures. I appreciate the opportunity to share with you some of what I have learned along the course of those journeys.

Fundamental #1:
Making Money

When I was growing up in the 1970s, I loved everything about television—even the commercials. I remember watching TV ads that in some cases were more interesting and entertaining than the shows that surrounded them. I watched as Coke taught the world to sing and taught Mean Joe Greene[2] to smile. I remember watching John Houseman in the advertisements for Smith Barney. "They make money the old-fashioned way," Houseman intoned. "They EARN it."

John Houseman died in 1988, and Morgan Stanley is planning to jettison the Smith Barney name at the end of 2012. But I like to think that Houseman and Smith Barney would be pleased to know that most of the wealth in America today is controlled by people who made and make the majority of their money the old-fashioned way: through hard work.

A hundred years ago, the richest Americans received only 20%

of their income from paid work. Today, that income proportion has tripled to 60%.[3]

How can you become one of those richest Americans? How can you become wealthy? I still believe what John Houseman and Smith Barney told me years ago. The most reliable way to make money is to earn it.

This is not a book about getting rich quick. My job as an investment advisor is to help my clients preserve, protect, and grow the wealth they have already earned. For the most part, my clients come to me **after** they have built a significant portion of their wealth, and my clients do not tend to rely on my advice regarding what the IRS would term "earned income."

However, I often have the opportunity to work alongside my clients as they experience continued success in their careers and as they counsel their children and grandchildren through the working world. So, in this chapter, I would like to share a few things I have learned along the way.

I believe that hard work is a necessary ingredient in achieving wealth. However, I also believe that hard work is primarily an outcome of successful choices rather than an input to those choices.[4]

I have been fortunate to know many successful people, and I always ask them how they built their wealth. That is an essential (and enjoyable!) part of my job.

No one has ever said to me, "When I was a child, I wanted to be as rich as I could, so I worked and worked and worked, and now I am."

On the other hand, I have known many people who have said to me, "When I was a child, I wanted to be the best doctor, computer programmer, engineer, pianist, football player, etc., I could, so I worked and worked and worked, and now I am."

Wealth often came as a natural byproduct of these successes—not always, but often.

Bill Gates did not spend his career focusing on how to get rich—neither did Steve Jobs, Mark Zuckerberg, or Sam Walton. Even those in the money trade—people like Warren Buffett, for example—did not get to where they are today because they wanted to be rich or because they worked hard to be rich. They all worked hard, for sure; they worked hard doing what they loved to do.

In a commencement address that Steve Jobs delivered at Stanford University in 2005, he expressed this idea simply, saying, "You've got to find what you love."

Perhaps Steve Jobs might not have become wealthy had he loved to teach or to care for animals or to counsel the elderly and the infirm. Steve wanted to build great companies and great products, and the market for those talents is robust and rewarding.

That said, Jobs focused on an interesting point in his speech at Stanford, recalling his days as a student at Reed College:

> *Reed College at that time offered perhaps the best calligraphy instruction in the country. Throughout the campus, every poster, every label on every drawer, was beautifully hand*

calligraphed. Because I had dropped out and didn't have to take the normal classes, I decided to take a calligraphy class to learn how to do this. I learned about serif and sans serif typefaces, about varying the amount of space between different letter combinations, about what makes great typography great. It was beautiful, historical, artistically subtle in a way that science can't capture, and I found it fascinating.

None of this had even a hope of any practical application in my life. But 10 years later, when we were designing the first Macintosh computer, it all came back to me. And we designed it all into the Mac. It was the first computer with beautiful typography. If I had never dropped in on that single course in college, the Mac would have never had multiple typefaces or proportionally spaced fonts. . . . Of course it was impossible to connect the dots looking forward when I was in college. But it was very, very clear looking backwards 10 years later.

Again, you can't connect the dots looking forward; you can only connect them looking backwards. So you have to trust that the dots will somehow connect in your future. You have to trust in something—your gut, destiny, life, karma, whatever. This approach has never let me down, and it has made all the difference in my life.[5]

Calligraphy does not present an obvious path toward great wealth, fame, and fortune—or a leadership role in technology. There are few high-powered, highly paid calligraphers in the world. However, there was something in that calligraphy class that combined in an important way with something in Steve Jobs. That something was part of how Jobs took Apple from near bankruptcy to its place as one of the world's most valuable companies. That something was part of what made Steve Jobs a billionaire many times over.

What if you are not Steve Jobs? What if you do not happen to be a superstar genius? Does the advice to do what you love, to follow your bliss, still hold?

I am not sure that advice still holds. Certainly, if you are a star—bright, talented, motivated, and personable—pursuing your talents and your passions is likely to pay off in whatever field you choose. However, I believe that it is important to be practical in your career choice, knowing that . . .

CAREER SUCCESS OFTEN LEADS TO FINANCIAL SUCCESS.

Take, for example, the well-meaning child who loves to play basketball more than anything in the world. If this child is both short and uncoordinated, then he—and those of us who resemble him in some form or fashion—may have a problem.

This child has probably been told to follow his dreams, to do what he loves, and the money will follow. More likely, if this child does what he loves, he will starve, at least if basketball is how he chooses to make his living.

Yes, some people do what they love, and the money follows. Millions more have followed their passion and still have not earned enough to pay back their student loans. One problem with following your bliss is that too many people want to work in the same professions—for example, in media, the arts, and non-profits. Employers in these fields get dozens if not hundreds of applications for each open position. Jobs are scarce, and due to the immutable laws of supply and demand, salaries in these fields are low. Opportunities for advancement in these professions are limited.[6]

At one point in my life, I thought I would make my living as a screenwriter. I love movies, and I thought I enjoyed writing. Someone told me that I should follow my passion and do what I love. The person who gave me this advice (with every good intention) spoke to me from the comfort of a beautiful Boston apartment, an apartment secured by his successful career in a most unglamorous industry.

Later in my life, I met a real screenwriter—several of them, in fact. I spent a few years in writing workshops. I discovered that I do not really enjoy writing; I enjoy having written.[7] Having a screenplay produced might be quite glamorous; however, waiting tables while hoping to be discovered as a writer is not much fun.

When I left the entertainment industry for business school, I told myself I would be more practical. A mundane job in a backwater industry might provide me with more opportunities to shine. Thousands of people wanted to write for the movies. How many wanted to be the director of manufacturing for the Ti-D Toilet Company?[8]

I figured at Ti-D Toilet—or in any less fictitious but similarly unglamorous spot—I would find reasonable work hours, kind treatment, opportunities for learning, and decent pay.

However, after two years of business school, I found myself again unable to focus on the practical and pragmatic. Sitting in my school's career center one day, I was reading through *National Geographic* when I found an article about a deep-sea diver who explored shipwrecks and looked for sunken treasure in oceans all over the world.

I was a NAUI-certified diver, and this sounded like the job for me. I called up the CEO of the treasure-hunting company profiled in the magazine, and I still remember what he told me: "First, get the *Good Housekeeping* Seal of Approval on your resume," he said. "Then you can go off on your adventures, and you'll always have the credentials to fall back on."[9]

At first, I was offended by this advice. After all, I already had not one but **two** Harvard degrees! How many more "seals of approval" did I need?

Ultimately, though, I followed through on the CEO's wise counsel. I took a job at McKinsey & Company, a well-known management consulting firm. It was another notch on my resume, another seal of approval.

After taking several opportunities to build and manage media and technology companies, I had done well for myself financially. I built a solid financial foundation for my family, which I credit to three things:

- I always enjoyed the work I did, which made working hard easier.
- I always worked hard.
- I had a good resume and a great network of friends and colleagues who would vouch for me (in no small part because I worked hard).

I did well financially but not so well that I was going to retire in my 30s. Temperamentally, I wouldn't have wanted to do that anyway, and I found myself in a bit of a funk.

I turned to my friends for advice. I hired a career coach. One of my clients introduced me to the writings of John Gardner, which inspired me. This particular passage from a speech Gardner gave to a group of young professionals at McKinsey & Company struck a nerve:

> *Not long ago, I read a splendid article on barnacles. I don't want to give the wrong impression of the focus of my reading interests. Sometimes days go by without my reading about barnacles, much less remembering what I read. But this article had an unforgettable opening paragraph. "The barnacle," the author explained, "is confronted with an existential decision about where it's going to live. Once it decides . . . it spends the rest of its life with its head cemented to a rock." End of quote. For a good many of us, it comes to that.*
>
> *We've all seen men and women, even ones in fortunate circumstances with responsible positions who seem to run out of steam in midcareer.*[10]

I looked at myself and where I was in my career. I had run out of steam. My head was cemented to a rock. I started signing off my e-mails, "Remember the barnacle!" which didn't make any sense to practically anyone other than me.

Then, I read an article by Herminia Ibarra that changed my life.[11]

I took an inventory of the things I liked to do and did well (and the things I did not like to do and did not do well).[12]

I interviewed dozens of people and tried to figure out what to do next. Ultimately, I found the perfect job for me—as a financial advisor.

I have come to believe that the key to career success is finding a job that is neither too difficult nor too easy. It is important to work for a company that you respect and for a boss who is kind and helpful. In addition, it is important to work in an industry that is growing rather than shrinking. Work with an organization whose business model scales and allows for a reasonable work/life balance. Look for a reasonable commute, good pay and benefits, and opportunities to learn and grow.

I have often found that financial success is built upon or enhanced by a successful career. Building a successful career is most easily accomplished if you love what you do.

However—and this is important—loving what you do is not the same as doing what you love. Many people confuse the two, but they are fundamentally different. Happiness as a byproduct of living your life is a great thing; happiness as a career goal can be a recipe for disaster.[13] If the only determinant of success were passion, then no cupcake business would ever fail.

Loving what you do is a necessary but insufficient condition for being successful at what you do. Being successful at what you do is a necessary but insufficient condition for becoming wealthy from the fruits of your labor.

My advice to those who are building their careers—those who are in the phase of their lives in which they are making money the old-fashioned way—is simple:

1. If you are exceptionally talented, then do what you love. If you are Steve Jobs, then go ahead and study calligraphy. Somehow, wealth will follow.

2. If you are someone of more ordinary abilities—like most of us—understand what you are good at (ability), what you like to do (passion), and what the world rewards (profitability). Build your career at the intersection of these three points. Two out of three does not get it done.

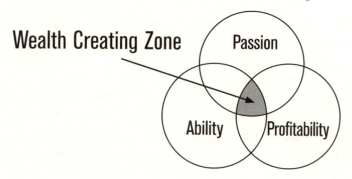

3. Watch out for things that meet only two of the three criteria listed on the prior page. Here is how you might view them:

   a. Things that you are good at and enjoy but do not pay well are hobbies.

   b. Things that you enjoy and pay well but you are not extraordinarily good at are hobbies (at least they are for you).

   c. Things that you are good at and pay well but you do not enjoy are traps. You will not work hard enough to succeed in a career that you do not enjoy no matter how good you are.[14]

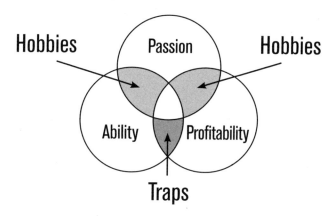

Find something that you are good at, you enjoy, and pays well. That is the first step to being financially successful.

However, there is more to financial success than simply earning

Fundamental #1

money. Before you can start investing the money you earn, you need to learn how to live within your means. Saving money is the next fundamental of financial success.

Fundamental #2:
Spending (and Saving) Money

As a financial advisor, I am limited in my ability to help my clients **become** wealthy. My clients are wealthy before they come to me for help, so my most important job is to help my clients **stay** wealthy. I help my clients preserve, protect, and grow their wealth over time.

I believe that the first fundamental principle of staying wealthy—and the second fundamental principle of financial success—is to spend less than you earn. To do that, . . .

YOU NEED A PLAN.

Why is planning around saving and spending so important—and so difficult? Because what you earn and what you spend change over time. If it were otherwise, planning would be easy. I could simply advise my clients to save some fixed percentage of their earnings, for example.

Life isn't that simple. There will be years when earnings and savings are high. There may be other years when spending is high and savings non-existent. For example, sometimes my clients forgo salaries while they start up new businesses; at other times, big expenditures may require spikes in saving and spending (for things like paying for children's education or buying a home).

The planning issues I confront are different for each client. Even if two individuals have a comparable amount of wealth and similar goals, their asset structures and tax situations may demand different planning considerations.

Every client is different, and every client needs a plan. Those plans should be flexible enough to accommodate each client's unique circumstances and goals.

WHAT IS YOUR NUMBER?

I always begin the planning process with each client by asking, "How much is enough?" What is the amount of money you need to set aside so you can be assured of maintaining your cash-flow needs without worrying as the years go by? Once you know your number, then you and your advisors can create an investment strategy to build and protect your wealth.

How can you know your number? That is the crux of the planning process.

Your plan should model best-case and worst-case scenarios regarding capital markets, inflation, and taxes to provide you with a high degree of confidence that the wealth you create—by spending less than you earn—will last a lifetime. That is your number: the amount you need to support yourself and your family even through the most difficult circumstances.

As an illustration, the table on the next page summarizes the output of some of my proprietary planning models. Regardless of who manages your financial plans, you should know what your numbers look like given **your unique circumstances**. Please do not use these or any other numbers as your guide. These numbers are here to illustrate a point and a process. In your planning, you should use numbers that directly and completely reflect your unique circumstances, goals, and constraints.

In the example that follows, I model the circumstances of a client who is 65 years old and spending $200,000 per year from his portfolio. Based on the table on the next page, I estimate that with a balanced portfolio composed of 60% globally diversified stocks and 40% intermediate-duration bonds,[15] this client needs to set aside $5.8 million to ensure he can withdraw $200,000 in real dollars from his portfolio every year for the rest of his life (after taking into account inflation and taxes).[16]

Of course, if you change any of these variables—age, spending rate, portfolio investment strategy, degree of confidence required—then your "magic number" changes. In other words, if $5.8 million seems like a lot—and it is—then there are ways to reduce this number, which will also naturally decline over time.

For example, let's assume I am sitting down with a client who is 45 years old and has already accumulated an investment portfolio of $1.5 million. Perhaps this client has pension and/or Social Security income that will generate $75,000 per year for him in retirement. Perhaps he also has rental properties that will generate $25,000 per year for him in retirement. If this client wants to spend $200,000 in retirement, beginning at age 65, he needs to save another $1.4 million. To reach this goal, he should save approximately $50,000 dollars each year for the next 20 years.

Annual Spending — **Core Capital Requirements by Annual Spending** [17]

Annual Spending							
$100,000	$3.5	$3.2	$2.9	$2.6	$2.3	$1.9	$1.6
$200,000	7.0	6.4	(5.8)	5.2	4.6	3.8	3.2
$300,000	10.5	9.6	8.7	7.8	6.9	5.7	4.8
$400,000	14.0	12.8	11.6	10.4	9.2	7.6	6.4
$500,000	17.5	16.0	14.5	13.0	11.5	9.5	8.0
$750,000	26.3	24.0	21.8	19.5	17.3	14.3	12.0
$1.0 Mil.	35.0	32.0	29.0	26.0	23.0	19.0	16.0

Core Capital Amounts ($ Millions)

Even in these simplified examples, there are a lot of moving variables. No one can be certain how investments will perform over the next 20 years, and no one can know how damaging or benign inflation will be—either in or ahead of retirement.

It is tempting to try to simplify planning—or avoid planning altogether—by using generic "rules of thumb."

Good planning should be customized to your individual circumstances. Generic examples can mislead.

For example, a recent article about retirement planning in *The New York Times* provided this rule of thumb: "To maintain living standards into old age, we need roughly 20 times our annual income in financial wealth. If you earn $100,000 at retirement, you need about $2 million beyond what you will receive from Social Security."[18]

A client showed me this article. His wife was upset after reading it. She was hoping to retire, and she hadn't saved anywhere near $2 million.

In this case, there was no need for her panic. I do not know what the author of *The New York Times* article was assuming about retirement age, but clearly, you need more money if you are retiring earlier in life and less if you retire later. It appears that the author was also assuming that retirees would have no income beyond Social Security. It is not clear to me what the author was assuming for Social Security (Full benefits? Spousal benefits? Both?). Most importantly, the author does not clearly describe what she is assuming about spending. After all, if someone spends less than he receives in Social Security (certainly unlikely in most cases, but just for the sake of illustration), then he would need **no savings** to retire once he begins receiving sufficient Social Security benefits. In this (extreme) case, a prospective retiree would not need a dime in savings, let alone 20 times his annual income.

My client was in good shape. She had pension and rental income, which covered most of her spending. She was worried for no good reason thanks to *The New York Times*. By providing her with a customized analysis reflecting her own unique circumstances, I was able to set her mind at ease.

Real life is full of uncertainty: salaries change over time, spending ebbs and flows, surprises happen. However, uncertainty should not be an excuse to avoid planning for your future. Rather, . . .

UNCERTAINTY MAKES GOOD PLANNING ALL THE MORE IMPORTANT.

Perhaps because uncertainty causes discomfort or perhaps because planning is hard work, surprisingly few people know their magic number: the amount of money they must save during their working lives to be assured of a comfortable retirement. Even fewer people are following a plan to get them to that number.

How do you create and follow such a plan? You should begin with a disciplined program of saving. There are no shortcuts for saving money even though all of us naturally wish there were.

Clients occasionally ask me how I can help them overcome a spending problem. "I don't want to spend less money," they will say. "What if you just earn more money on my investments, and I'll spend that!"

Unfortunately, great investment management can rarely offset poor budgetary discipline. Here is an illustration. Let's say you have already saved a million dollars.[19] At that point, if you were to choose a particularly skilled investment manager who could help you outperform the markets by 1% a year, that extra 1% would net you an extra $10,000 (1% of $1,000,000). So, I suppose, that is $10,000 per year that you would not need to save—all else being equal.

However, outperforming the market by "just" 1% year after year is **really** hard. Fewer than 20% of all investment managers can generate this level of performance over long periods of time.[20] On top of that, most clients who have a "spending problem" have a problem that is much bigger than $10,000 per year. Generally, the more money you make, the more money you spend.

If you are spending too much money, then you almost certainly will not be able to work your way out of that problem by hiring a different investment manager or by asking him to invest in assets that generate a higher level of return. Rather, . . .

THE ONLY SOLUTION TO A SPENDING PROBLEM IS TO SPEND LESS MONEY.

Unfortunately, I need to have these kinds of spending discussions with some clients. These are not conversations anyone enjoys. Clients never thank me for telling them they need to cut back on their spending, but my job is to give clients prudent advice even if they do not want to hear it.

Sometimes, in these situations, clients ask me how they can spend less money and where they should cut back. Although this is not my area of expertise, I can offer my opinions. I have the benefit of not just one lifetime of experience (my own) but of many lifetimes of experience (my clients'). Here is what I've learned:

- A big house can be a big headache. More houses can create more headaches.

- Tangible goods can last longer than intangible experiences. However, for many people at many points in their lives, the joy they receive from what they experience can outweigh and outlast the joy they receive from their purchases of tangible things.

- A series of several small indulgences can sometimes provide more joy than one or two big purchases.

- Some people prefer to pay now for things they can look forward to enjoying later; others prefer the reverse. It can be helpful to know what you prefer (and, if you are married, what your spouse prefers).

- There are times (such as right now in the fall of 2012) when credit is so cheap that borrowing money to create investment leverage can make sense for some investors. On the other hand, some people sleep better at night if they have less debt.

- Spending less than you earn isn't necessarily easy, but (for most of us) it is essential to long-term financial success.[21]

In the first chapter of this book, I noted that clients don't often come to me for career advice, nor do they tend to come to me for the advice I have given here on how to build wealth through better approaches to saving and spending.[22] Nonetheless, I have my opinions. Your mileage, as they say, may vary.

I can help my clients understand how much money they can afford to spend, and I can create an investment portfolio that properly matches my clients' changing spending levels and liquidity needs.

I am poorly equipped to tell clients what they should trim from their budget or where and how they should spend additional funds. Everyone's preferences are different.

It may give me great joy to contribute to my favorite charity, and I might rather give up a few fancy dinners than cut back on my charitable contributions. Someone else might feel exactly the opposite way.

You might sleep quite well with a first, second, and third mortgage on your home. I would not. I make no moral judgment with regards to how my clients spend their money. I simply pass along my own experiences and opinions and try to provide my clients with the facts they need to evaluate their own options and opportunities.

Finally, in closing this section, I'll mention another article I read recently in *The New York Times*.[23] The story posed the question of how much money people need to be happy.[24]

The data here is murky. This particular article in *The New York Times* claimed that additional income doesn't buy additional happiness once a certain comfortable standard of living has been met. Other studies[25] have shown that while the marginal utility of additional income declines with income, income can continue to have a positive impact on levels of happiness.

All the articles I have read support this point: having enough money to pay your bills now and in the future is likely to make you happier than worrying about whether your checks are going to clear.

Making sure that you plan to have enough money is the topic of my next chapter on building a bulletproof financial plan.

Fundamental #3:
It Is Easier to Get There If You Know Where You Are Going

Understanding the impact of the financial choices you make is difficult because the future is unknown.[26] However, just because you can't be certain of what the future holds, doesn't mean you can't plan for the future. A good investment plan incorporates the probable outcomes of different investment strategies and provides a pathway to achieve your most important goals with the highest degree of probability.

Investors can't do anything about the markets—and, for that matter, the unpredictable twists and turns in their personal lives are often not entirely in their control. Investors have the most control over four crucial aspects of their financial plans:

- When they choose to retire.
- How much they spend.

- How they allocate their portfolios.
- How they put taxable and tax-exempt accounts to best use.

Despite the unknowns, investors and their advisors can create tailored, long-term plans that are stress-tested for weathering even the most hostile markets.

No plan, however, should be static or unchangeable: the markets and each investor's unique circumstances will almost certainly change if a plan is in place for any length of time. Therefore, good plans must evolve.[27]

The key to successful planning is a framework that carefully quantifies the likely outcomes of different strategies in different markets. Some outcomes are highly unlikely because they are so strong and others because they are so weak. Other results are more typical. Every investor should consider the unlikely (positive and negative) as well as the likely. To put it simply, . . .

GOOD PLANNING LEADS TO GOOD DECISIONS.

Here's an illustration.

A few years ago, a couple came to me with a question. He was 50 years old and miserable in his job. She was miserable living in the city and wanted to retire to their farm out in Virginia. They both wanted to know when he could retire so they could move back home to the country.

At the same time, she was nervous about money. She considered herself to be a conservative investor—nearly everything the couple owned was in bonds, cash, and precious metals. She didn't like to spend money: they were fighting about country club dues and the money he wanted to spend building a pond and a new set of stables on their property.

I am not a marriage counselor, but I can tell you this: building and maintaining a financial plan was one of the best things these clients—let's call them Jim and Mary Turner[28]—ever did for their marriage.

My colleagues and I built a series of models based on different retirement dates for Jim, different spending patterns, and different investment allocations. We looked at how the Turners' portfolio would perform in good markets, bad markets, and "normal" markets; how inflation would impact their plans; how changes in the tax code might affect them; and how they could utilize different planning strategies to make sure they were taking care of their children and giving to charities in tax-efficient ways.

At the end of this process, we defined a set of clear tradeoffs. Jim and Mary could continue to invest their assets conservatively (as Mary wanted), and they would have little risk of ever running out of money even if high inflation and low growth ravaged their portfolio—provided, of course, that Jim kept working for a long time and they kept their spending in check.

Alternatively, a more aggressive asset allocation would allow for an earlier retirement **or** some of the spending on capital improvements that were important to Jim—but not both.

Fundamental #3 | **31**

In later conversations, Jim told me he had been upset with Mary because he had assumed it was her approach to investing that was preventing him from achieving his financial goals: more spending and an early retirement. He was surprised to learn that there was **no** prudent investment approach that would allow him to retire early and spend such a large fraction of his savings each year.

Mary was surprised to discover that adding some investments she considered "risky" (e.g., stocks) to their portfolios could protect her against inflation. Such investments would allow her to move back to the farm quite a bit earlier without significantly adding to the risk or volatility of their overall portfolio.

Both Jim and Mary were relieved to know they could accomplish all of their goals—retiring to the farm in a reasonable timeframe; spending a comfortable amount on their lifestyle; and investing in a portfolio that reflected an appropriate, understandable, and tolerable tradeoff between risk and return.

Our planning process was—and is—a dynamic one. Jim, Mary, and I have met several times in the past few years, and we have adjusted their plan when circumstances intervened. We've had new and unexpected expenses pop up (e.g., problems at the farm and loans to some of the Turners' children) and had unanticipated additions to the portfolio (e.g., the sale of another investment property and income from a board seat Jim accepted). So, we make course corrections on the portfolio and on household budgeting as circumstances change.

One thing is clear: it is easier and safer to get to where you are going (in this case, retirement in the Virginia countryside) if you have a roadmap to help guide you.

It is also worth remembering that investment goals and plans can be about more than money. Planning can be an expression of your values. For example, in addition to making sure your children are financially secure, you can also use the planning process as part of the way you express some of your values to your children and grandchildren.

In many cases, a good financial plan is a multigenerational plan. For many of my clients, their planning process is designed—in part—to inspire their children to achieve success in their own right and to continue philanthropic pursuits that are important to the family.

Before I leave the topic of financial plans, I want to show you how to evaluate the various mixes of assets that are a part of your investment choices. As we consider different asset-allocation possibilities, we necessarily find ourselves in a discussion of risks and returns.

GOOD PLANNING REQUIRES AN UNDERSTANDING OF RISK.

Financial advisors sometimes say that riskier investments produce higher returns or, conversely, that if you want to generate higher returns in your portfolio, then you need to take more risk.

This risk/return tradeoff gets repeated so often that most people don't realize that it doesn't make much sense. After all, if an investment reliably produced higher returns, then, by definition, it wouldn't be higher risk.

A more precise way to describe the relationship between risk and return is this: assets that produce higher returns on average also have a greater dispersion of returns around their average return. In other words, investors choose between assets that have relatively lower but more certain returns and assets that have relatively higher but less certain returns.

This definition of risk explains how assets are priced. Investors demand higher returns to invest in assets whose return patterns are more volatile or less certain. This definition of risk adequately describes risk from the perspective of the investment, but how should investors think of risk?

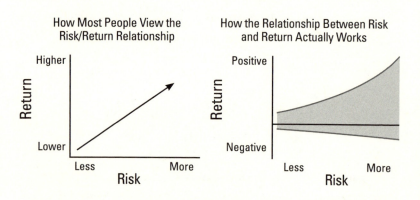

For the investor, the most important risk is not volatility or less certain returns. For the investor, the most important risk is running out of money. Each investor has different needs, and failing to meet those needs presents the most important (and entirely unique) risk in each investor's financial life.

For example, a retired executive may need his portfolio to return 4% or more each year in order for him to pay his bills without dipping into his principal. A younger worker may need his retirement fund to grow by 7% on average to secure the retirement he anticipates, and a prolonged period of 5% returns would entail serious risks for this young worker. These risks are personal and unique to each investor. Any given investment may present risks to one investor's financial plan and be riskless for another investor who is differently situated.

Similarly, illiquidity presents different risks for different investors. If an investor needs money to pay taxes or buy a home in a year, then he may not be able to make an investment that ties up his money beyond that deadline. For this investor, risk isn't just about the potential to lose money or about volatility; risk is about being unable to turn an investment into cash at a reasonable price at a specific moment in time.

Underperformance represents a third kind of risk, a risk that impacts investors and investment professionals psychologically as well as financially. The psychological dimension of underperformance risk is rarely understood outside the investment industry, but it is an important factor to consider as investors hire and evaluate investment managers.

If an investment manager believes that his clients will not accept returns that are below benchmark returns for a given asset class, he may be tempted to emulate the benchmark index. After all, if this manager's portfolios don't look like the benchmark does, the manager is almost certain to generate some periods of underperformance. Many of the best investors have the courage to stick strongly to their approach even—and especially—when markets move against them. Because no approach works 100% of the time, these investors can experience significant periods of underperformance.

For example, in the late 1990s, Warren Buffett and other value-oriented investors dramatically underperformed the stock market. This underperformance was rewarded in the following years as value stocks performed much better than the market as a whole. Buffett was able to take on benchmark risk—or underperformance risk—because his investors were patient and willing to tolerate this risk.

If you aren't willing to take on benchmark/underperformance risk, then you shouldn't hire an active investment manager—not even one as good as Warren Buffett. Instead, you should buy low-cost, passive index funds. Many investors pay active managers who "hug the benchmark" because these managers are afraid their clients will leave them if they ever underperform. However, eliminating the risk of underperformance also necessarily eliminates the possibility of superior performance. You don't need to pay the higher fees active managers require if you want index-like performance.[29]

The quality of investment decisions and the risks associated with them cannot be determined simply by looking at prior performance—even though this is exactly how investors tend to evaluate investments and investment managers. For example, a portfolio that was perfectly positioned against 99% of market outcomes can perform poorly and, therefore, look like it was a risky investment if the other 1% of outcomes occurs. Similarly, a portfolio that was designed to do well in 50% of all market scenarios and do poorly in 50% of all market scenarios can look deceptively safe if you track performance only after the desired developments materialize. A wildly speculative portfolio that will fail spectacularly in 99% of all markets can be mistaken for a perfectly conservative portfolio if that one unlikely outcome happens to occur.

Safety comes from an investment approach based on solid value and valuations—not investor sentiment. It doesn't come from any single asset or asset class but from a well-designed and well-maintained long-term strategy tailored to each investor's unique goals.

Finally, the fourth type of investment risk is what financial advisors often call risk tolerance. Personally, I believe that risk tolerance is not a particularly helpful way to define risk. Risk, after all, has many dimensions. All investors are infinitely tolerant of the risk that an investment might increase in value. Fewer investors are tolerant of the risk that an investment might decrease in value.

One of my colleagues refers to risk tolerance in the context of a choice between eating well or sleeping well. He references the choice between two investments—one with a high degree of risk and another with lower, more certain returns.

"If you want to dine well," he says, "invest in the first. If you want to sleep well, invest in the second."

You and your investment manager should discuss the level of risk and the types of risks you are willing to take with your investments. This is an important part of understanding what different investment mixes to consider when creating your financial plan.

Fundamental #4:
What You Keep Is More Important Than What You Earn

As an investor, it is important to understand the impact of taxes, inflation, and fees on your wealth. You should understand how different investments, investment managers, and market conditions influence these costs. At the end of the day, what matters is not what you earn but what is left over after the government and everyone else has taken their cut.

As an illustration, let's look at the effects taxes and inflation can have on wealth. For instance, we can begin by looking at the returns posted by stocks and bonds between 1967 and 1986 and again between 1987 and 2006 (please see the table on next page).

The Impact of Taxes and Inflation on Returns[30]

1967-1986 Annualized

	Bonds	Stocks
Return	8.4%	10.2%
Taxes	(2.7)	(1.9)
Inflation	(6.2)	(6.2)
Real After-Tax Return	**(0.5)%**	**2.1%**

1987-2006 Annualized

	Bonds	Stocks
Return	6.9%	11.8%
Taxes	(1.5)	(1.3)
Inflation	(3.1)	(3.1)
Real After-Tax Return	**2.3%**	**7.4%**

Interestingly, the nominal results for both bonds and stocks were strong in both periods. However, the combination of higher taxes and much higher inflation eroded results significantly in the earlier 20 years—significantly enough to bring the real after-tax return on bonds into negative territory. The latter two decades were far more benign.

Note that you would have rather experienced a 6.9% nominal pre-tax return on your bonds from 1987 to 2006 (resulting in an after-tax real annualized gain of 2.3% per year) than an 8.4% nominal pre-tax return on your bonds from 1967 to 1986 (when that same return resulted in a real after-tax loss of wealth).

Sometimes, a 6.9% return is more than an 8.4% return. Counterintuitive? No, not when taxes and inflation are factored in.

You cannot control inflation or the tax rates that governments levy. You can, however, do something about taxes and inflation if you understand how and why they matter to you as an investor. We will come back to inflation in a moment, but let's start here…

TAXES MATTER. THE MONEY THAT YOU SEND TO THE GOVERNMENT COMES OUT OF YOUR POCKET.

My clients are concerned about the taxes they pay on the income they generate from their jobs and their portfolios. My clients are concerned about the capital gains taxes they pay on the growth of their investments. They are also concerned about the gift taxes they pay and the estate taxes that might be levied after their death. Ultimately, even if I do a good job protecting and growing my clients' wealth, I am not doing them any favors if we give up too much of that wealth to the government.

Tax management of a taxable investment account should be a continuous process—not just a series of tax trades at the end of the year. My research shows that the most basic tax-management strategy—avoiding short-term gains and deferring long-term gains until you are convinced that realizing those gains is worth the tax penalty—adds approximately three-quarters of a percentage point to your after-tax return each and every year.

Potential Added Return from Tax Management (Annualized) [31]

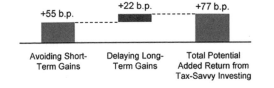

With my clients, I focus on prudent tax management designed to complement—not dominate—our investment process. Taxes are often my clients' single largest investment cost—larger than fees, commissions, and custody charges taken together. Whenever I can decrease the amount of taxes my clients have to pay, I can increase the wealth my clients get to keep—as long as I don't sacrifice too much pre-tax return. My goal is not simply to reduce my clients' tax burdens but to maximize their after-tax returns.

The popular concept of tax efficiency (the percentage of a portfolio's pre-tax return an investor gets to keep after taxes) only goes so far. Sometimes, it may be better to keep less of a higher pre-tax return than more of a lower return.

I stay mindful of subtleties like these when managing my clients' taxable accounts, paying special attention to stocks because tax-exempt municipal bonds are always available for purchase. In all cases, I work closely with my clients' tax advisors and provide reports to ease income-tax reporting in even the most complex situations.

Even for the same client, I manage taxable stock accounts differently from tax-exempt and tax-deferred accounts by employing a range of techniques:

- All else being equal, selling higher-cost purchases first—rather than those bought earliest—so realized gains will be smaller.

- Avoiding short-term gains except where holding an asset is unusually risky or where an extraordinary buying opportunity justifies paying a tax penalty.

- Harvesting losses—if economically justified—using strategies to avoid abandoning assets whose return potential is still substantial.

- Buying Treasury and other taxable bonds in municipal bond accounts when the yields on those bonds are high enough after taxes.[32]

- Avoiding purchasing mutual funds close to when year-end distributions would expose clients to a tax bill on shares only recently acquired.

- Quantifying the tradeoff between holding on to a highly appreciated stock that forms a large portion of a client's portfolio and biting the tax bullet for the sake of diversification.

- Evaluating tax effects in allocating assets between taxable accounts and tax-deferred accounts like IRAs.

Gift and estate taxes also play an important role in determining family wealth. Once my clients and I have determined their core capital needs—the amount of money they need to secure their own lifestyle over time—we can focus on the "excess" capital that could otherwise be consumed by taxes. We create multigenerational plans to find the best ways to build and transfer wealth to the people or charities my clients care about most.

After all, there are only four things you can do with your money:

- You can spend it on yourself.

- You can give it to your children, grandchildren, and/or other important people in your life.

- You can give it to charities or other important causes in your life.

- You can give it to the government in the form of taxes.

I work with Democrats and Republicans—clients across the political spectrum. Some willingly pay the taxes they owe while others resent every dollar they have to pay. All my clients have one thing in common: none of them want to pay any **more** taxes than they are legally obligated to pay. On the list of ways to spend your money that I have provided above, no one seems to like the last option best.

To keep your taxes to a minimum, you and your investment manager need to keep track of many moving parts, including your personal tax profile, the tax characteristics of your assets, and the types of accounts in which your assets are held. A good investment manager should think about taxes every day and should monitor each trade for its tax consequences in order to seek the best after-tax return for his clients.

In managing your accounts, your investment manager should work closely with your tax advisors to stay on top of your tax situation, watching for gains or losses that may occur outside the accounts they manage, alternative minimum tax liabilities, opportunities to use tax-loss carryovers, ways to minimize taxable gains through loss harvesting, and opportunities to save on taxes based on life transitions or tax-code changes.

If that sounds complicated, well, it is.[33] It isn't easy to manage for after-tax returns. It is also almost impossible to compare one manager to another on an after-tax basis. With both of these complexities in mind, many investment managers simply don't bother to focus on taxes at all.[34]

In part because focusing on taxes doesn't help brokers win business, many brokers don't optimize their clients' tax planning. However, taxes should matter to you. You should discuss tax management with your financial advisor regularly.

Investors also are wise to remember that...

INFLATION MATTERS.

In addition to taxes, you also need to be aware of how inflation can take a big bite out of your investment portfolio.

As the chart on the next page demonstrates, inflation spikes are rare. There have been only three significant spikes in inflation over the past 110 years.

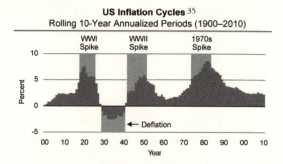

Though rare, inflation spikes can be extremely damaging to investors. Traditional stock/bond portfolios have historically lost purchasing power during inflationary periods, as shown in the chart below.

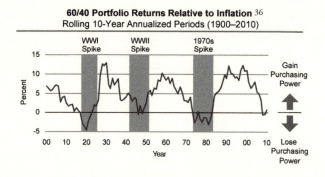

However, most investment portfolios are not designed with inflation risk explicitly in mind. As a result, many investors are often dangerously susceptible to an unexpected rise in inflation, which can present one of the most pernicious environments for traditional investment portfolios. What's worse, at the same time that many investors' assets are hit by an inflationary spike, their liabilities and living costs also tend to rise. Such a double whammy can leave investors in a deep hole.

There is a good deal of confusion and disagreement about how best to protect an investment portfolio against inflation. Financial experts disagree both in terms of what assets hedge inflation most effectively and how to incorporate them into a portfolio.[37]

Because every investor has unique liabilities and portfolio objectives, there is no single inflation-protection formula that is right for all investors. Instead, investors should simply be aware that . . .

REAL RETURNS ARE WHAT REALLY MATTER.

Your approach to inflation should depend on your unique financial circumstances. Some investors have liabilities (e.g., adjustable-rate mortgages) that increase with inflation. These investors have a greater need for protection against inflation spikes. Similarly, investors whose income is positively linked to inflation— for example, investors who have pensions linked to cost-of-living adjustments or who own properties that produce rents that can be increased in an inflationary period— have less need for inflation protection than those whose income is not linked to inflation. In every case, inflation can significantly influence your investing experience. Your investment strategy should carefully consider how inflation can affect you.

Finally, in addition to inflation, . . .

COSTS MATTER.

Costs matter to everyone, but many investors take an exceedingly narrow view of the costs associated with their investments. This narrow view can disadvantage them as investors.

To be sure, the investment industry does everything it can to make it as difficult as possible for investors to understand—let alone compare—the costs they face. Fees are charged in dozens of different ways: when you first put money into an investment, on an annual basis, and/or when you take money out of an investment. Some providers charge commissions or other fees on transactions while others do not. Some charge by the hour. Some charge a percentage of assets under management. Some do all of the above in various combinations.

These fees are described in tiny print inside long disclosure documents that few investors ever read. When these fees change, you get new copies of those documents in the mail, and you probably read the new documents every bit as closely as you read the original documents. You should ask your investment manager to explain and account for the fees charged to you. After the explanation, ask again if those are **all** the fees associated with your account. Chances are, there are a few more that haven't been mentioned.

Now, there is nothing inherently wrong with fees. Your investment advisor is doing an important job, and he deserves to be paid for doing that job well. What is frustrating to me—and to many of my clients—is how hard it is to understand exactly who is being paid what.

Here is an example.

At my firm, we charge a flat fee to manage a bond account. That fee is based on the size of the account. So, we might charge $5,000 (0.5%) to look after a $1 million bond account over the course of a year.

I had a client come to me and tell me that he found a firm that would manage his bonds for free. It was a special deal, he said, because this firm wanted to earn his business.

The first thing I did was look up some of the names of the people who ran this firm's bond research department. I also found the names of some of the bond traders the firm employed.

I couldn't find the salaries of these people on the company's website or in any financial statements, but I did find the employees' addresses in the phone book. I took my client on a tour of some of the nicest real estate in Long Island and Connecticut.

"This is where the folks who manage those bonds live," I told him. "Do you wonder how they can afford those homes when they don't make any money?"

Of course that firm was being paid to manage bonds for its clients! The firm wasn't charging fees, and it wasn't charging commissions. Instead, it was marking up each bond that it bought and sold. So, if the firm bought a bond at $1.06, it might pass the bond along to the firm's clients at $1.08.

There is nothing wrong with marking up bonds in this way—it is perfectly legal and appropriate—but it is not free.

As difficult as it can be to understand what fees are being collected and how those fees are being charged, it is also exceedingly difficult to compare, for example, whether you are better off with a firm that is charging you a commission versus a fee versus a markup. In practice, most firms are charging you a combination of all three, in addition to other costs. Making a comparison on costs is almost impossible.

Unfortunately, many banks and brokerages seem to believe that complexity and obfuscation work to their advantage. By making things opaque, these companies hope to build a more profitable business for themselves.

You might be tempted to give up trying to understand all these fees and choose to manage your money yourself. I don't think it is wise to face the markets alone, and in a moment, I'll explain an easy way to evaluate the fees you are being charged in the context of your investment performance (even if your investment manager doesn't want you to know what you are paying him). But first, a thought or two on managing your money on your own.

Certainly, you can manage your own money. You can also file your own taxes, prepare all your own meals, and act as your own representative in court. I don't do or recommend those things, but you certainly could.

I prefer to have an accountant who stays current on IRS rules and regulations, which change all the time. I could teach myself how to cook Japanese, Thai, French, and Chinese food, but I would rather spend my time doing other things, and I enjoy eating out.

Before signing a contract, I like to have someone who studied jurisprudence and spends thousands of hours each year in the practice of law review that contract with me.

I have a degree in economics and another in business administration. I suppose I could figure out what stocks I want to own, when to buy them, and when to sell them, but I don't.

I prefer to have people—hundreds of analysts—who spend every minute of every day figuring out what stocks and bonds to buy and sell on my behalf. I prefer to have dozens of other experts who are looking at the tax ramifications of those trades and are keeping an eye out for risks like inflation and market volatility.

The cheapest solution—doing it yourself—is not likely to be the best solution, which brings me to my final point in this chapter . . .

VALUE AND COST AREN'T THE SAME.

As I previously described, it can be exceedingly difficult to understand what fees, commissions, markups, etc., you are being charged by your investment manager. If your goal is to find the person who charges you the least, then that would be a problem.

Finding the lowest-cost investment manager shouldn't be your goal, and that's why this isn't really a problem (even though the complexity of some financial service firm's fees can be frustrating, unfriendly, and—in my mind—unethical).

To illustrate this point with an analogy, let's say I have two babysitters who are available for hire. One charges $10 per hour and the other charges $5 per child. Which one are you going to employ?

The first question you could ask might not be about the sitters' respective costs. Isn't it more important to know which of the two is better with younger or older children? Whether one drinks? Has a prison record? Spends all night on the phone or watching TV?

As Albert Einstein famously said, "Everything that can be counted does not necessarily count; everything that counts cannot necessarily be counted."

If you want to count things up anyway, you can—sort of. Fortunately, you can account for fees without counting them— as confusing as that might sound. What you really care about is what your investments have earned **after** all fees are taken into consideration. To determine those earnings, just look at your account balances from one year to the next, and don't forget to net out your capital additions and withdrawals over the course of the year (you would be surprised how many people forget about that).

Your goal should be to find the investment manager who—**after** all taxes and fees are accounted for—will do the best job for you. If you give this person $1,000, and one year later the account stands at $1,100, well, you earned 10% after all fees. I don't know what those fees were, and you probably don't either. Maybe your investment manager doesn't even know. But, whether those fees were commissions or markups or whatever, after all is said and done, you're $100 better off, and that is the number that should matter most to you.

While there is a lot more to understanding how taxes, inflation, and fees can impact your investments, this chapter should at least provide you with a basis for discussing these considerations with your financial advisor. Please do your research and ask a lot of questions. Most importantly, please don't give up on the investment plan you and your advisors have put into place. If your wealth is growing according to that plan, then you are counting what really counts. Einstein would be proud of you.

Now let's change gears once again and focus our attention on the fifth fundamental of financial success: diversifying your investments and the benefits that diversification provides.

Fundamental #5:
Diversify Your Investments

You have some money to invest. You have talked with your financial advisor about taxes, inflation, and costs. You know your number (see Chapter 2), and you and your financial advisor are building your investment plan together. Now a question arises: in which assets should you invest to best achieve your goals? The first and best piece of investment advice that anyone can give you at this stage of your process is to . . .

DIVERSIFY.

But, what, exactly, does diversification mean?

Let's look at an example. I once had a prospective client, John, who told me he learned the importance of diversification the hard way.

In the past, John had all of his money invested with one investment manager. This manager had done well for a period of time—that is, until John suffered disappointing losses in his portfolios.

"I learned my lesson," John told me. "Now I have seven different investment managers."

I took a deep breath. There are some good reasons to use multiple investment managers, but diversification usually isn't one of them.[38]

I asked John for a copy of the statements these seven managers sent him each month. My first reaction was, "Wow, that's a lot of paper!" I'm not sure John was really keeping track of what these managers were doing for him. If he had wanted to keep track, it wouldn't have been easy. Each month, John was getting more than a hundred pages of financial statements, and his was not a particularly large or complex account.

My first challenge was to see what John's managers had bought for him. For the most part, these managers had all bought mutual funds—several different mutual funds—because John had told them he wanted to be diversified.

Now, it is possible that all seven of John's new managers could have bought John the exact same set of mutual funds. If they had, then clearly John would not have been any more diversified than he would have been with a single manager. Having seven people each buy A, B, and C for you is no more diversifying than having one person who buys seven times as much of A, B, and C for you.

As it turns out, that wasn't exactly John's problem, but it was pretty close to his problem. Indeed, John's problem was harder for a casual investor to discern.

You see, each of John's seven investment managers had invested in different funds, all with different names. This looked great on paper until John and I examined what the funds owned. As it turned out, each fund owned the same handful of technology and telecommunication stocks.

In total, John owned a few dozen funds that were being managed by seven different managers. Nearly every fund John owned held large positions in the same four or five stocks. Even though no single mutual fund made up more than 7% of John's holdings, he had nearly 20% of his money invested in just ten stocks.

Because these stocks were being bought by dozens of different mutual fund managers and these mutual funds were being held in seven different brokerage accounts, no one was able to help John decide whether or not he should own so much of these stocks. John was less likely to benefit from diversity at the single-stock level because he had created meaningless and valueless diversity at the mutual fund and manager level. So, the lesson here is . . .

DIVERSIFICATION MATTERS, BUT WHAT YOU DIVERSIFY MATTERS MORE.

I asked John why he had so many different managers and so many more mutual funds. He told me that he didn't know whom to trust. With that in mind, I reminded John of the cautionary tale of Chicken Little and Henny Penny.

A Cautionary Tale

Chicken Little heard that you shouldn't put all your eggs in one basket. So, she carefully placed her eggs in seven beautiful baskets that she lined up neatly on the kitchen table in front of her before falling soundly to sleep. When she awoke, Chicken Little found the table had tipped over, the seven baskets had fallen to the ground, and her eggs were all broken.

Henny Penny put all of her eggs in one basket. Instead of spending her time dividing up eggs among different baskets, she spent her time evaluating the baskets, choosing the one that was right for her, and then watching her eggs in their basket very, very carefully—ensuring that her nest eggs wouldn't break.

Figuring out whom you can trust in the world of finance is no easy matter. Financial service companies don't make it any easier. In fact, many banks and brokerage companies fight tooth and nail against any rule or regulation that would provide greater transparency or consumer protection.

However, the challenge of evaluating different advisors is no excuse for throwing up your hands and giving up. Choosing seven different financial advisors because you are not sure which one of them might be a crook or an idiot is not a good approach. Consider being more like Henny Penny—investing your time before you invest your money. Do your research. Ask your savvy and discerning friends for referrals. Find someone whose investment approach makes sense to you. Choose one basket carefully and then watch that basket carefully.[39] After all, this is your nest egg we're talking about.

Diversifying your investments by hiring several different investment managers or by buying several different mutual funds is **not** what I mean by diversification.

Moreover, having multiple investment managers has real costs:

- Many investment managers charge a percentage fee, which declines as the amount of assets they manage for you increases. In other words, if you have $1 million to manage, you will pay more to have two managers (each of whom manages $500,000 of your money) than you will to have one manager (who manages $1 million of your money).

- Your time is valuable. Meeting with two different investment managers and coordinating and compiling their statements and reports takes twice as much of your time as it does to meet with and manage one investment advisor.

- Coordinating multiple investment accounts over multiple investment managers makes tax management exceptionally difficult.

Find one investment advisor. Make sure he is someone you trust, and make sure he is someone worthy of your trust.

Fundamental #5

There are three basic components of effective diversification:

- Diversify across different asset classes.
- Diversify across different geographies.
- Diversify across different investment styles.

Diversification is difficult because it runs against our every instinct. When something (e.g., real estate, gold, emerging markets, growth stocks) is doing well, we want to own more of that thing. When something isn't doing well, we want to own less of that thing.

As an investor, you should fight this instinct with every fiber of your being. Failure to do so may be hazardous to your wealth.

The chart below illustrates another important benefit of diversification. Different assets perform differently at different times. No one—not even the best investors—can perfectly predict how the performance of any given asset class will change over time.

Major Markets: Annualized Returns [40]

	1981–84	1985–86	1987–88	1989–91	1992–96	1997–99	2000–11
Best Performer	REITs* 19.5%	Foreign 62.7%	Foreign 26.4%	Emerging 33.1%	Value 17.3%	Growth 34.1%	REITs 11.8%
	Bonds* 15.1%	Value 25.6%	Emerging 26.3%	Growth 24.2%	REITs 17.1%	Value 18.8%	Emerging 8.1%
	US Value Stocks* 14.5%	Growth 23.8%	Value 11.3%	Bonds 13.1%	Growth 13.4%	Foreign 15.7%	Bonds 6.5%
	Foreign Stocks* 6.2%	Emerging 20.0%	Growth 8.2%	Value 12.8%	Emerging 12.7%	Bonds 5.7%	Value 3.3%
	US Growth Stocks* 5.3%	REITs 19.1%	Bonds 5.3%	REITs 7.7%	Foreign 8.2%	Emerging 3.2%	Foreign 0.6%
Worst Performer	Emerging Markets* (7.7)%	Bonds 18.6%	REITs 4.6%	Foreign (1.7)%	Bonds 7.0%	REITs (1.8)%	Growth (1.9)%

Changing market environments are simply a given in investing. No asset class, geography, or style always finishes first or brings up the rear, and it is impossible to predict which will post the best returns. As the table on the previous page demonstrates, foreign markets performed well from 1985–1988 and then poorly over the next three years. Similarly, real estate underperformed in the late 1990s but did extraordinarily well in the following decade (even considering the spectacular real estate crash in 2008).

The case for diversifying widely is simple in theory: this way you are certain to capture a portion of any outperformer's returns each year while muting the impact of any underperformers.

Like asset classes, countries also take turns leading and lagging in the markets (as shown in the figure on the following page). Returns from each stock market around the world ebb and flow, and the fortunes of countries throughout the world shift—often abruptly and unpredictably. Market-timing strategies are of little use (and are often counterproductive) in trying to navigate this fast-moving global maze.

No Country Always Wins... or Loses [41]

	1996	1997	1998	1999	2000	2001	2002	2003	2004	2005	2006
Best Performer	Spain 50.2%	Italy 57.5%	Italy 42.3%	Singapore 101.3%	Australia 6.0%	Australia 10.4%	Australia (10.3)%	Hong Kong 37.5%	Sweden 25.9%	Japan 44.6%	Singapore 35.5%
	Sweden 41.4%	Spain 47.0%	Spain 39.4%	Sweden 89.4%	Italy 5.3%	Spain (6.5)%	Singapore (16.4)%	Germany 36.3%	Australia 25.3%	Sweden 32.1%	Spain 33.6%
	Hong Kong 33.1%	Germany 45.3%	France 31.4%	Hong Kong 60.1%	France 2.2%	UK (11.8)%	Hong Kong (17.8)%	Sweden 35.9%	Hong Kong 25.1%	Germany 26.7%	Hong Kong 30.7%
	France 28.8%	US 33.4%	US 30.1%	France 51.4%	UK (4.5)%	US (12.4)%	Japan (18.8)%	Singapore 34.7%	Italy 22.9%	France 26.6%	Sweden 23.3%
	US 23.2%	Sweden 31.2%	Germany 19.9%	Japan 46.6%	Germany (9.9)%	France (18.1)%	Italy (21.4)%	Spain 31.8%	Spain 19.6%	Australia 24.0%	Australia 21.8%
	Germany 22.3%	France 29.5%	UK 16.5%	Germany 40.6%	Spain (10.2)%	Germany (18.2)%	US (23.1)%	US 28.4%	Singapore 17.5%	Spain 20.3%	Germany 21.6%
	UK 15.6%	UK 27.5%	Sweden 16.4%	Spain 22.8%	US (12.8)%	Singapore (18.5)%	UK (23.4)%	Japan 22.7%	UK 11.5%	UK 20.1%	France 20.3%
	Australia 9.1%	Australia 9.2%	Australia 12.7%	US 21.9%	Sweden (13.1)%	Hong Kong (18.6)%	Spain (28.1)%	UK 18.8%	Japan 10.8%	Italy 17.4%	Italy 18.5%
	Italy 7.9%	Japan (14.5)%	Hong Kong (2.9)%	Italy 16.8%	Hong Kong (14.5)%	Japan (19.0)%	France (33.1)%	France 16.7%	US 10.1%	Singapore 16.5%	US 15.8%
	Japan (4.9)%	Singapore (15.7)%	Japan (8.9)%	UK 16.1%	Japan (19.8)%	Sweden (19.0)%	Sweden (42.3)%	Italy 14.7%	France 9.9%	Hong Kong 8.1%	UK 14.6%
Worst Performer	Singapore (7.9)%	Hong Kong (23.2)%	Singapore (14.7)%	Australia 10.3%	Singapore (24.8)%	Italy (22.6)%	Germany (43.3)%	Australia 11.7%	Germany 7.8%	US 5.1%	Japan 7.3%

Also, like asset classes and countries, different investment styles go in and out of fashion. Investors may be tempted to shift assets from their growth portfolios, for example, to their value portfolios when value is poised to outperform and vice versa. However, while this may be emotionally appealing, in practice, it is not.

The best way to capitalize on shifting cycles is to maintain your long-term strategic asset allocation—by asset class, geography, and style. Remember Icarus? Try to avoid flying too close to the sun or the sea. It is often most prudent to choose the middle course—diversification—and stick to it.

The goal of diversification is to own assets that perform differently at different times. By owning a diversified blend of assets, you are likely to experience a smoother ride through the markets. With a smoother ride through the markets, you are more likely to be able to stick with your investment plan. Sticking with your investment plan is a surer path to success than chasing returns.

However, owning a diversified collection of assets doesn't mean you should own every asset. Not all assets are created equal. Some offer higher returns than others, some have more risk than others, and—importantly—some offer more diversification benefits than others. The trick is to find the collection of assets that when taken together, offer the best tradeoffs between risk and return. The trick is to find the assets that are the best diversifiers to one another.

Here we find one of the first counterintuitive lessons of investing. Although cash is a safe asset on its own, as part of a diversified portfolio, cash does not offer the most safety for investors.[42] That's because . . .

BONDS OFFER BETTER DIVERSIFICATION THAN CASH.

I have seen investors make the mistake of favoring cash over bonds many times. When investors are worried about the equity markets, they often want to hide out in cash. However, I always advise my clients to consider that during down stock markets, bonds' benefits are far superior to those of cash and its equivalents. When stocks drop sharply, anxious investors tend to pull money out of the equity markets—almost always unwisely—to put their funds into cash and bonds for safekeeping. Bonds are a better bet because they counterbalance stocks' volatility far better than cash does. Bonds rise in price as investors pour money into them, generating gains that can help offset stock losses.

The real lesson here is not that you should turn to bonds instead of cash when stocks start to tumble. The real lesson is that you should have a significant allocation to bonds at all times. As an investor, you can never predict when or for how long stocks will decline.

After reading this chapter, you may have a different understanding of the importance of diversification and what diversification really means. Now, let's take a closer look at how you might choose among and between different assets as you invest according to the goals set out in your investment plan.

Fundamental #6:
What You Buy Matters More Than Who Buys It for You

One of my clients invests half of his money with me and half of his money with another investment firm. Every six months or so, we seem to have the same conversation.

"Tell me how much money you made for me over the last six months," he asks.

"Okay," I usually answer. "Why?"

"So I can see how well you're doing against the other guy," he says.

This is a minefield. If I am not careful, I might give my client factual but extraordinarily unhelpful information—information that could lead him to make bad decisions. Unfortunately, these are exactly the kinds of bad decisions that too many investors make too often.

The money I manage for this client is invested differently from his other money. For example, most of the money I invest for this client is in non-taxable accounts or tax-deferred accounts while most of the money his other manager invests is in taxable accounts.

As a result, in the accounts I manage for this client, I purchase taxable bonds. In my client's other accounts, his other manager buys municipal bonds.

Both managers are doing exactly the right thing for this particular client, but when I report my bond returns, they are almost always going to be higher than the returns the other manager reports because (tax-advantaged) municipal bonds usually pay lower (pre-tax) returns than do taxable bonds. On an after-tax basis, things even out, but neither I nor this client's other investment manager report after-tax returns. We can't. Every family's tax situation is different, and the full effect of taxes in any account can't be calculated until after a tax return is prepared.

A manager who is managing taxable bonds will often outperform (on a pre-tax basis) a manager who is managing municipal bonds. I am always careful to point out to my clients when they are comparing apples to oranges and not making a fair comparison across managers.

Please don't think that every investment manager works this way. Many, unfortunately, are always looking to find ways to paint their numbers in the best light and to make their competitors look bad. If you are not comparing the exact same time periods, the exact same asset allocations, and the exact same tax situations, then you aren't going to be able to make a valid comparison among and across managers.

When clients are evaluating my firm against other managers they might hire, they often ask this question: "How did your firm perform against the indexes and against other managers over the last year (or three or five years)?" That's a good question to ask, but only as part of a broader conversation about asset allocation because…

ASSET ALLOCATION MATTERS MORE THAN MANAGER SELECTION.

To illustrate, let's imagine that you are talking to two different financial planners, and for simplicity's sake, let's assume there are only two assets you can buy: stocks and bonds.

The first planner works for Stockpicker Incorporated (SI). You ask him how his firm has performed over the past five years. "We're the best in the business," Mr. Stockpicker tells you. Just look at our performance:

Year	Stock Benchmark[43]	SI Stocks	Bond Benchmark[44]	SI Bonds
2007	5.5%	6.5%	3.1%	3.6%
2008	-37.0%	-36.0%	-1.2%	-0.7%
2009	26.5%	27.5%	8.5%	9.0%
2010	15.1%	16.1%	2.0%	2.5%

Each year, SI's research analysts have been brilliant at choosing stocks and bonds. Each year, they have outperformed the stock

Fundamental #6 | **67**

market by 1% (in their stock funds) and the bond market by 0.5% (in their bond funds).

Now, you go across the street to Long-Term Planners (LTP). You ask the same question. Here's what the planner at LTP shows you:

Year	Stock Benchmark[45]	LTP Stocks	Bond Benchmark[46]	LTP Bonds
2007	5.5%	4.5%	3.1%	2.6%
2008	-37.0%	-38.0%	-1.2%	-1.7%
2009	26.5%	25.5%	8.5%	8.0%
2010	15.1%	14.1%	2.0%	1.5%

LTP has underperformed its relevant benchmarks by 1% per year (in stocks) and 0.5% per year (in bonds).

So, which firm should you choose to manage your money?

Choosing an investment manager solely on the basis of that manager's ability to outperform a benchmark is likely to lead you to imperfect investment decisions (at the very best).

Suppose, for example, that in 2007 and 2008, SI had its clients invested heavily in stocks while in 2009 and 2010, SI had its clients invested heavily in bonds. Also, suppose that LTP recommended just the opposite for its clients.

It is quite possible that you would have done much better with LTP than with SI. For example, if you had invested $100,000 with SI in a portfolio that was 60% stocks/40% bonds in 2007 and 2008 and 40% stocks/60% bonds in 2009 and 2010, you would have a portfolio worth $103,580 at the end of 2010.

If you had invested that same money with LTP, allocating 40% stocks/60% bonds in 2007 and 2008 and 60% stocks/40% bonds in 2009 and 2010, your portfolio would have been worth $112,115 at the end of 2010. LTP would have earned you more than three times as much money even though their benchmark performance was worse than SI in every asset class and in every period.

Investors' preoccupation with alpha—defined as any given manager's ability to outperform an index and/or his peers—goes a long way toward explaining why most investors have lagged the market over the last 20 years.

Just as investors tend to focus too narrowly on alpha when evaluating asset managers, investors also tend to focus too narrowly on past performance when evaluating asset classes. Focusing on past performance reinforces investors' tendency to chase recent winners and dump recent losers. This leads to buying high and selling low, which can throw investors badly off course and destroy a lot of their wealth.

The following chart shows how U.S. mutual fund investors behaved over the last 15 years. Excited by the spectacular gains in the technology sector in the late 1990s, they added $140 billion to U.S. equity mutual funds in the first quarter of 2000 and were then pummeled when the bubble burst in March of that year.

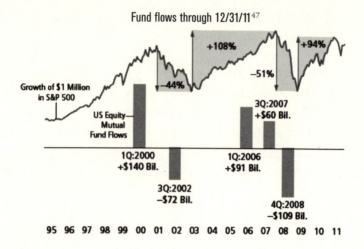

Chastened, investors exited stocks over the next few years, withdrawing $72 billion in the third quarter of 2002 alone—just when the market hit bottom, 44% below its early 2000 peak.

Over the next five years, the equity markets more than doubled, and investors piled back into equities. They invested $91 billion in stocks in the first quarter of 2006 and another $60 billion in the third quarter of 2007—just in time to be clobbered by the 51% drop after the credit crisis hit.

True to form, investors pulled $109 billion out of U.S. equity mutual funds in the fourth quarter of 2008 only to miss the 94% run-up that followed over the next two-and-a-half years.

Given this perverse tendency to buy high and sell low, investor outcomes can be poor even when markets are strong. That is just what happened over the past 20 years, as shown in the next display.

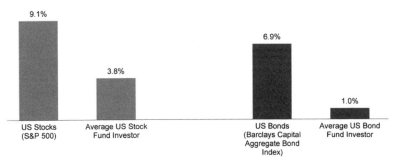

Annualized Returns[48]
1991–2010

While the S&P 500 returned 9.1% per year on average from 1991 through 2010, the average U.S. stock fund investor earned just 3.8% per year. While the municipal bond market returned 6.9% per year on average, the average U.S. bond investor realized almost none of those gains.

Investors tend to sell funds that have recently performed poorly and buy the "hot" funds that have recently done well. Most investors end up buying high and selling low when it comes to managers and when it comes to asset classes. The results are the opposite of what investors desire.

A second problem with focusing on alpha and prior performance is that the metric for annualized returns assumes no additions or withdrawals from principal over time. Almost no one invests this way.

Most investors experience cash inflows and outflows over time, which can have a huge impact on their investment outcomes.

The display on page 73 provides a vastly simplified example, based on someone with no savings who invests $10,000 at the

Fundamental #6

beginning of each of three consecutive years. First, let's suppose high returns come first: the markets return 25% in the first year, are flat in the second, and lose 20% in the third. The investor ends up with $26,000—well below the $30,000 he started with.

If the sequence of returns were reversed so that the low returns came first, the average return would be the same. In other words, the average of 25%, 0%, and -20% is the same as the average of -20%, 0%, and 25%.

However, while the average return would be the same, the investor's experience would be quite different. He would end up with $35,000—well above the $30,000 he invested.

Why? Large investment gains and losses have a much greater impact on your long-term results if they occur after several years of saving, when you have more assets. In this example, just reversing the sequence of returns increases the investor's final outcome by 35%.

Here is another example (also illustrated on the following page): an investor who starts with $100,000 and withdraws $10,000 at the beginning of each of three years. If the high return (the 25% gain) comes first, the investor ends up with $74,000. If the low return (the 20% loss) comes first, he ends us with $65,000—or 12% less. That is because market losses have a bigger negative impact on final outcomes at the beginning of the spending phase, when you have more assets to lose, and market gains have a smaller positive impact later, when you have fewer assets.

With Cash Flows, the Sequence of Returns Drives Outcomes

$ Thousands

Savings Phase
(Starting with $0 and adding $10k per year)

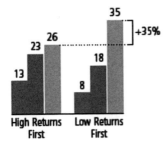

Withdrawl Phase
(Starting with $100k and withdrawing $10k per year)

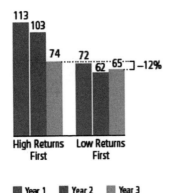

In short, the annualized returns generated by asset classes and asset managers fail to capture the most important truths about investor experiences. A focus on annualized returns can encourage performance chasing and have a pernicious impact on investor behavior. Investors need a better way to assess performance.

I believe that performance should be viewed through the lens of planning. Your investments are performing well if you are on target to meet your investment goals. It is that simple. I call that target "core capital."

CORE CAPITAL MATTERS MOST OF ALL.

I first referenced the concept of core capital in Chapter 4. As discussed in that chapter, core capital is simply the amount of money investors need in order to have a high probability of meeting their spending requirements over time. Focusing on core capital can help investors build sound investment plans and make appropriate midcourse adjustments as their circumstances change.

The display below provides a schematic diagram of core capital.

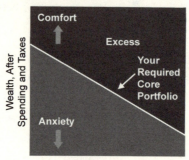

The core line represents all of the points at which there is a high likelihood that the investor will meet his financial goal. The line slopes downward over time because the total amount of money an individual needs declines as he ages and has fewer years of future spending to fund.

At any point in time, the goal is to stay above the core capital line. Being above the core capital line places an investor in the comfort zone. The further below the core capital line an investor's portfolio strays, the more anxious he should feel.

Investors' core capital requirements are different depending on their time horizon, spending needs, and tolerance for variability in their net worth along the way. For simplicity's sake, however, let's consider one hypothetical example: a professional couple, both age 60, whom we might have met in 1995.

This hypothetical couple was planning to retire and spend about $100,000 in current dollars each year for the rest of their lives. My analysis would have shown that they would have needed about $2.6 million to support their spending over the rest of their lives.

The couple's actual net worth was somewhat lower—about $1.8 million. However, they had a long time horizon, and my analysis showed they were close enough to their core capital goal to have a good chance of closing the gap. The couple decided to go with a middle-of-the-road 60% stock/40% bond allocation to take advantage of the growth potential of equities without subjecting themselves to undue volatility along the way.

So, how did they do? Initially, the couple would have benefited from the bull market of the late 1990s, with their net worth growing substantially in excess of their core capital needs by 1999. This can be seen in the chart on the following page.[49]

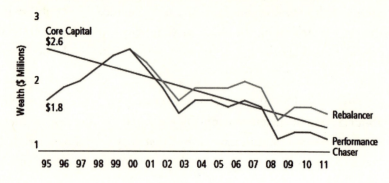

Actual Wealth vs. Core Capital for Two Hypothetical Investors

If the couple rebalanced their accounts annually—trimming assets that were doing well and buying more of whatever was lagging—they would have seen performance over the following years as illustrated by the upper line ("Rebalancer"). This rebalancing couple would have maintained their 60/40 allocation in good equity markets and in bad. Rebalancing is the key to buying low and selling high (and rebalancing is so important that it is the subject of the next chapter). Rebalancing is the opposite of what most individuals do.

Our hypothetical performance chaser would have increased his exposure to equities at the end of 1999, near the height of the tech bubble. As a result, he would have lost more than our hypothetical couple (who rebalanced), and his portfolio would have fallen further below the core capital line.

After two years of terrible market returns, the performance chaser would have reduced his target equity allocation, which would have hurt his ability to benefit from the equity market rebound that began in 2003. Consequently, the performance chaser's portfolio would have barely risen above the core capital line in 2006.

Determined to gain more from the equity market rebound, the performance chaser would have increased his equity allocation in 2006 and 2007—just in time to be clobbered by the market drop in 2008. Traumatized by that experience, he would have cut his target equity allocation at the end of 2008 and missed the huge market rebound that followed.

The performance chaser's portfolio value would have significantly underperformed the rebalancer's portfolio. Most importantly, the performance chaser would have fallen further and further behind his core capital number over time, putting his own financial future at significant risk.

While the bad behavior and poor results of our hypothetical performance chaser may seem extreme, I based the timing and direction of his asset-allocation decisions on the big shifts that were made by mutual fund investors as shown on the display on page 70. The graph on page 73 shows the effect of comparatively modest asset-allocation shifts. Many real-world investors moved their asset allocations much more in response to market swings.

Finally, our hypothetical performance chaser maintained the same mix of growth and value stocks and of U.S., developed international, and emerging market stocks throughout the time period. He didn't shift managers, trying to chase alpha. Many real-world investors chase the performance of styles, geographic markets, and managers, and their performance is all the worse for it.

In short, investors who are aggressive in chasing performance often fare poorly. Investors who focus on core capital rather than annualized return have a much better measure of success in meeting their investment objectives.

Of course, you would like to find an investment manager who is good at **both** security selection (i.e., outperforming a benchmark) **and** asset allocation. Unfortunately, all managers outperform in some years but not in others; every manager outperforms in some asset classes but not in others. The data are complex and hard to compare across managers, across asset classes, and across time.

Yet, one thing is certain…

GOOD PLANNING AND GOOD ASSET ALLOCATION TRUMP SECURITY SELECTION EVERY TIME.

This is because even the best managers outperform their benchmarks by a relatively small margin, as the figure below demonstrates.

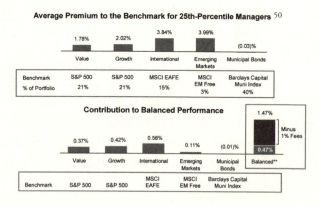

If you were able to choose some of the best managers in each of the five different asset classes shown in the illustration on the prior page, then you would have outperformed the benchmark by less than one-half of one percentage point per year.[51]

While the value of alpha is relatively small, the difference in performance across asset classes is relatively large. Stocks, for example, have outperformed bonds by about 2.2% per year over the last 20 years,[52] and in individual years, stocks have outperformed bonds by 10% or more ten times while bonds have outperformed stocks by 10% or more in four of the last 21 years.[53]

Being in the right asset class at the right time is much more important than which manager you choose to manage any given asset class.[54] What you buy matters much more than who buys it for you. I can tell you from personal experience this is not how most investors choose their managers, and they are often poorer for it.

To reach your full financial potential, it is important to reevaluate your financial plan continually and rebalance your asset allocation over time. In the next chapter, I'll talk about exactly how to do that.

Fundamental #7:
You Are Already Off Course

As I described in Chapter 3, investors, like other travelers on life's journeys, are more likely to get to where they are going if they have a destination in mind. It is not enough just to have a plan; in addition, you need to stick to that plan.

In investing terms, we call the course corrections that we all make on life's journeys "rebalancing." And . . .

REBALANCING IS AN ESSENTIAL PART OF STAYING WITH YOUR PLAN.

One thing I do for clients is establish an appropriate band around their strategic asset allocation. I then rebalance their portfolios back toward their strategic target when their asset mix hits the band. For example, with a 5% band, I would rebalance a 50/50 mix of stocks and bonds when either component hits 45% at the bottom or 55% at the top.

A technical note—I would go back only 50% of the way. So, for example, if stocks outperformed and hit that 55% top band, I wouldn't take stocks back to 50%. Instead, I would reduce my client's equity exposure to 52.5% because the incremental costs of taxes and transaction costs associated with further rebalancing would be greater than the benefit.[55]

If you owned only two assets—say, stocks and bonds—then rebalancing would be relatively easy. However, if you own more, then things get more complex. With three assets (stocks, bonds, and real estate), there are three rebalancing points (stocks/bonds, stocks/real estate, and bonds/real estate). With seven assets (U.S. stocks, international stocks, emerging market stocks, bonds, real estate, commodities, and currencies), there are 12 rebalancing points, and there are additional rebalancing points within each asset class. For example, within your U.S. stock portfolio, some stocks will be performing well and others less well at any given point in time.

Rebalancing is difficult but worthwhile. My research indicates that a properly rebalanced portfolio is likely to return an additional 0.3% per year compounded.[56] That may not sound like a lot in percentage terms, but here is what it means in dollars: $1 million invested for 30 years in a properly rebalanced portfolio will earn you about $94,000 more—about 10% more money— than the exact same portfolio without rebalancing.

Rebalancing sounds simple and mechanical, and it is. It also has a wonderful benefit when put into practice: rebalancing forces investors to do one of the most difficult things that investors do. It forces them to buy low and sell high.

One of the most fundamental rules of investing is to buy low and sell high, but buying low and selling high is exceedingly difficult to do in practice. Emotionally, every instinct we have pushes us in the opposite direction. It feels good to buy what has already gone up in price, and when something costs us money, we want to get rid of it—quickly.

Just look at gold. Investors seeking safety pushed the price of gold up close to $2,000 per ounce in 2011, triple its level just five years earlier. Gold is a volatile asset with poor long-term returns. Many people who were buying gold in 2010 and 2011 felt gold was a safe investment in part because the price of gold had appreciated so dramatically during a period of market uncertainty. However, is it really safe to buy gold—or anything else for that matter—when it is priced near an all-time high?

After adjusting for inflation, gold has delivered negative returns in 58% of all rolling 10-year periods since 1971—far worse than stocks or bonds. Even more astonishing, gold's purchasing power[57] declined 20% or more in 47% of all rolling 10-year periods.

Similarly, 10-year U.S. Treasuries have lost purchasing power in 12% of the 10-year periods since 1971, and in half of those cases, the loss in the purchasing power of Treasuries was 20% or more. Because Treasuries pay a fixed interest rate in nominal[58] dollars, they can lose purchasing power when inflation rises more than investors expect.

Like other crowded trades where most investors are on the same side, the lingering mania for gold and Treasuries following the financial crisis of 2008 was a self-fulfilling prophecy in the short run. Ultimately, however, crowded trades always reverse.[59]

The paradox of risk and crowded trades works both ways. I have heard investors say they would not buy a particular asset at any price because the asset was simply too risky. However, when everyone believes something is risky, then investors' unwillingness to buy that asset can reduce prices to the point where the asset presents little risk at all. A high-quality asset can present a lot of investment risk if it is purchased at too high a price, just as a low-quality asset can present wonderful investment opportunities if the asset is purchased at a significant discount to its intrinsic (as opposed to perceived) value.

We know that we need to buy things **before** they go up in price and sell them **before** they go down in price. However, because we can't see into the future, we tend to look in the rearview mirror. Rearview-mirror investing can be extraordinarily destructive to your wealth.

Rebalancing forces you to stick with your investment plan, and if you stick with your plan, then you are likely to do well. Rebalancing forces you to buy investments before they go up in price, increasing the odds that you will maintain your core capital (as described in Chapter 6).

For example, let's assume that you retired at the worst possible time in the last 100 years—in 1929. You were invested in a 60% stock/40% bond portfolio, and you needed to spend 4% of your initial portfolio (growing with inflation each year) to support your lifestyle. With the stock market crash of 1929, you would have quickly fallen to a level where your assets would have been insufficient to guarantee your spending for the rest of your life. As markets improved, however, you would have been back to a place of financial comfort by 1935 and would have remained there for the rest of your life, as shown in the figure below.

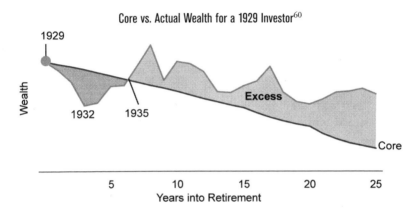

Of course, this only would have happened if you stuck with your plan—rebalancing back into stocks as they were declining from 1929 through 1932.

To use a more current example (in the figure on the following page), let's say you retired in 1999. First, you would have made a little money, then lost a little money, made a little money, and so forth. Ultimately, by the end of 2011, you would have ended up with 10% more money than you needed to support your spending in retirement even though you lived through two of the worst bear markets in history—the bursting of the tech bubble in the early 2000s and the credit crisis a few years later.

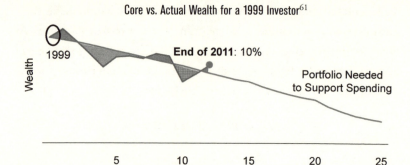
Core vs. Actual Wealth for a 1999 Investor[61]

Again, your plan would have worked even in 1929 and 1999—two of the worst markets in history. But your plan will work only if you work your plan. Rebalancing is an essential part of working your plan.

In these two examples, you can see how powerful a financial plan can be. Planning is important even (and especially) when an investor lives through exceptionally difficult times, such as the Great Depression, the bursting of the tech bubble, and/or the global credit crisis of 2008.

These kinds of difficult times are **exactly** when investors with the discipline to stick to their plans are most rewarded. Imagine how difficult it was to buy stocks in 1932, 2002, or 2009—**after** stock prices had declined so significantly. Imagine how difficult it was to sell your bonds and your other "safe" investments in those environments. On their own, few investors had the courage or the foresight to do so, but rebalancing forces us to buy on the dips and sell on strength.

Rebalancing reinforces our financial plans through each and every market cycle. Taking your grandfather's advice—to buy low and sell high—is harder than it looks. Rebalancing makes these purchases and sales easier by making them an **automatic** function of your investment plan.

However, rebalancing isn't a cure-all. The examples I have provided should not suggest that you can always count on rebalancing to make your plans succeed. Success depends on other factors as well, including your accumulated wealth, your budget, and your time horizon. Your objective should be to develop a plan that provides you with enough money to secure the rest of your life, your legacy, and your charitable goals. Then, you need to maintain your plan with vigilance and a programmatic approach to rebalancing.

If you want the best chance of succeeding with your financial plan, then you should be slow to make judgments based on short time spans—even ones as calamitous as the early years of the Great Depression.

My first seven chapters outlined how you might go about creating and implementing a financial plan customized to your unique circumstances. I do not believe you should build and implement this plan alone. You will be best served with a financial advisor to guide you through the investment process and help manage your portfolios. Your advisor should help you build your financial plan and help you stay the course as your financial life unfolds.

In choosing an advisor—a partner on the journey outlined in your financial plan—you should evaluate several different and important factors carefully. The last three chapters in this book describe what you might want to take into account when you choose your financial advisor.

First, we'll look at the various sources of information available to you as an investor.

Fundamental #8:
The Source of Information Matters

One problem with the financial media—whether we are talking about CNBC; *Fortune*; *The Wall Street Journal*; or any other cable television network, magazine, or newspaper—is that they are not in the investment advisory business.

The personalities on CNBC and the writers in *The Wall Street Journal* don't make more money or have better job security if they do a good job providing investment advice to you or anyone else. Newspapers and magazines (and their employees) are in the business of selling newspapers and magazines. The media business is the business of building ratings, readership, or viewership to generate as much advertising revenue as possible. Being in the media business, rather than the investment advisory business, means these writers, journalists, and entertainers have every incentive to tell stories and present information in ways that will keep you—and as many other people as possible—watching and reading.

Being a part of the media world doesn't make these people bad or unethical; it just makes them a terrible place to turn for investment advice.

Which story do you think commands more viewers or readers: a well-reasoned and nuanced evaluation of the economy or an interview with someone who is predicting that the world is going to come to an end?

What makes for better copy—an article about prudent financial planning or an article about the guy who found an investment that went up 1,500% last year?

One of the fundamental principles of economics is that markets are more efficient if there is a free flow of information. However, I know that as my clients spend more and more time absorbing much of this information—watching CNBC, for example, or monitoring their portfolios on a minute-by-minute basis on the Internet—they are far less likely to be successful in sticking to their long-term investment plans. At the same time, these media-saturated clients are much more likely to suffer stress and anxiety in the short-term.

As investors, we cannot control the markets. We can control how we choose to react to the markets. Being reactive—rather than proactive—is likely to destroy wealth. Being focused on short-term market movements rather than long-term fundamentals is likely to destroy both your wealth and your peace of mind.

Also, please remember: just being on TV doesn't make anyone an expert. Similarly, success in the markets over the past few years isn't proof of wisdom, competence, or insight. In the foreword, I noted the cautionary tale of Charles Mackay—the brilliant financial journalist who wrote the preeminent textbook on market bubbles and then got caught up in the British railway stock bubble a few years later. Here is another story from 150 years later to illustrate that same point and to demonstrate the dangers of following so-called "experts" on the basis of recent past performance.

In 1994, Orange County, California, declared bankruptcy—the largest municipal bankruptcy in recent history.

However, before Orange County declared bankruptcy, it was a shining beacon of success for other city managers and investors—many of whom borrowed money to join its investment pool.

Few bothered to ask Orange County's treasurer, Robert Citron, how he was generating such phenomenal returns. Citron wasn't shy about answering. If you had asked, he would have told you he was consulting a mail-order astrology service to guide him in making investments. But no one was asking.

When interest rates spiked, Orange County landed $1.64 billion in debt. Citron pleaded guilty to six felonies, and the county had to lay off more than 1,000 employees.

So, what does this story reveal? Don't take investment advice from people just because they happen to be famous. Don't take investment advice from people just because you see them on TV or because they have published a book.[62] Don't take investment advice from people just because they've done well over the past few years. Good investment advice is customized to you and your unique situation. If advice is being broadcast to millions of viewers or published for millions of readers, then that advice is clearly not targeted to you. If advice worked for someone else in the past, then that is no indication it will work for you in the future.

With so many potential sources of information at hand, how can you find someone who can give you good, customized investment advice? Here are four things you might consider:

- **Credentials:** If you find the alphabet soup of financial certifications confusing, then you are not alone. Some certifications take years of study and experience to attain; others take only a weekend course and an open-book exam. What credentials should you look for when choosing a financial advisor? Look for a firm that includes Chartered Financial Analyst® (CFA) charterholders among their researchers and Certified Financial Planner™ (CFP®) certificants among their planners. Both designations require a university degree, several years of relevant professional experience, a rigorous exam process, and continuing education. Both designations entail strict ethical and professional standards.

- **Fiduciary Standard:** Many advisors have to follow only a suitability standard, meaning the investments they sell to you merely need to be suitable for you and are not necessarily in your best interest. The suitability standard also does not require disclosure of conflicts of interest. A Registered Investment Advisor (RIA) is a fiduciary with a legal obligation to put your best interests first and to disclose all conflicts. Do not accept a suitability standard. This is crucial and should be a deal breaker. Do not hire a prospective advisor who is not a fiduciary to you.

- **Independence:** Brokerage firms and insurance companies are in the business of creating and selling financial products. Asking them for financial advice is like asking a Mercedes salesman whether you should buy a new Mercedes. Instead, look for an independent firm that offers objective advice. Ask for a fee-based, pay-as-you-go structure that is not influenced by transactions or commissions.

- **Outsourcing:** As the old saying goes, "Those who can, do; those who can't, don't." Find an experienced firm that makes investment decisions for its clients rather than outsourcing money management to third parties. This is a good way to separate true practitioners from those simply acting as middlemen. The closer you are to the people who manage your money, the more likely you are to get the outcome you anticipate.

I will end this chapter with a story and some personal advice. My daughter, Elizabeth, loves to sing. Mostly, what she sings makes absolutely no sense. For example, in her nursery school class, the teachers have been asking all the children to line up in alphabetical order. Elizabeth has turned this into a song. "Alphabetical order!" she sings. "ALPHAbetical order. AlphaBETICAL order! Alphabetical ORDER!"

The same words repeated over and over . . . Those words don't make any sense in the context of Elizabeth's song, if you stop to think about them. Still, she's charming, so I'm glad to listen.

When your four-year-old daughter is talking nonsense, sometimes you can forget that what she's saying is nonsense. That is okay; she is your four-year-old daughter.

When someone on television is talking nonsense, that might be a different story. Less charming, potentially every bit as seductive, and a whole lot more dangerous. So, remember . . .

BE CAREFUL OF WHERE YOU GET YOUR INFORMATION.

Beware of charming people spouting nonsense. To find someone who is speaking sensibly, you might start by looking for a financial advisor who will keep your best interests in mind. Finding a financial advisor whose interests are aligned with yours is the subject of the next chapter of this book.

Fundamental #9:
Get Financial Advice from People Whose Financial Interests Are Aligned With Yours

Yesterday, I overheard my two sons talking at the dinner table. Robert, who is in fifth grade, was explaining something he had learned in math class to James, who is in first grade. The topic was percentages. Robert decided to use money as a way of explaining the concept.

"Let's say I loan you $10," Robert said, "and I charge you 10% interest every month. How much would you owe me at the end of the month?"

James wasn't paying any attention.

To Robert's credit, he immediately changed tactics.

"Let's say there is a great set of Pokémon cards that you want to buy," Robert said. "It's got every card ever made. Level X, Prime, Legend, and even Holographic," he said.

I have no idea what any of those words mean, but James' eyes were now wide open and fixed squarely on Robert. "Wow," James said. "That would be great!"

"So the Pokémon cards cost $100," Robert continued, "but you don't have any money, so I loan you the $100, and you'll have to pay me $120 when you get some money next month. That's 20% interest because $20 is 20% of $100."

As Robert continued, he did a pretty credible job of teaching James about interest and percentages. What did he teach me?

- First, I think Robert might make a pretty good financial advisor one day.

- Second, if you want to explain something to someone, talk in his language—not yours.

- Third, never borrow money from your older brother. 20% interest? Per month?!

You will—and you should—talk to various people who hold themselves out as financial advisors. Some of these people will be lawyers, some accountants, and others will be insurance salespeople, stockbrokers, or registered investment advisors. These people will have lots of initials after their names: CPA, LLM, JD, CFP, CFA, MBA, ChFC, CLU, PFS, and so on. Some of these initials have value and relevance; many do not. Some of these people will be smart and helpful; others will not. Most, if not all, of these people will be ethical and well-meaning, but few will have your best interests at heart. Being able to understand their motives is essential to protecting your interests.

Remember what I learned from listening to Robert: don't borrow money from your brother. Don't get distracted by his fancy talk about Pokémon cards. Pay attention to the numbers.

How might you translate these lessons in your search for an advisor? I would suggest that you shouldn't take financial advice from someone whose interests don't align with your own. Don't get distracted by his fancy talk. Pay attention to the numbers.

I have come to believe that investment management is both a profession and a business. It is important to understand how these two frames of reference—professional obligation and business operations—influence practitioners and their clients.

The profession of investment management should be about doing what is best for investment clients. The business of investment management can be about doing what is best for investment managers.

In this respect, investment management is no different from law, architecture, medicine, accounting, consulting, or anything else. There is often a struggle between the values of a profession and the economics of the associated business. Values and economic interests can be in direct alignment. When investment managers build trust with clients, they can build a valuable business. In the long run, building a business depends on building a reputation for ethical, excellent behavior.

In my experience, however, there are many practitioners in the investment business who don't have a long-run perspective. In the short-run, these people are looking out for their own interests, not the interests of their clients.

What can you do to protect yourself? First, . . .

FOCUS MATTERS.

The business of investment management is like many other businesses in that greater scale can produce higher profits. There is a temptation for banks and brokerages—just like other businesses—to get bigger, and for consumers, there are benefits to "one-stop shopping" in financial services just like there are anywhere else. It might be more convenient, for example, for you to have just one relationship with someone who can offer you a checking account, a brokerage account, insurance, and other financial products you need.

However, there are two problems with this "one-stop shopping" model. First, I would rather have two people helping me who are each expert at their jobs rather than have one person helping me who is mediocre at both of his.

The other problem with this model of "one-stop shopping" is that multiple lines of business can create conflicts of interest—or, at the least, potential conflicts of interest—between clients and the companies who advise them.

For example, if your financial manager is also responsible for underwriting stock and bond issues, how do you evaluate his "buy" recommendation on a stock for your portfolio? If he is selling stocks or bonds to you out of his own inventory, how can you feel comfortable buying something that his company is selling (or vice versa)? If your financial advisor gets differing rates of commissions on different products—for instance, if he gets paid more to sell insurance than to have you keep money in your checking account—how do you evaluate his recommendation to take money out of your checking account to buy insurance?

One way around these problems is to look for advisors who have focused businesses, who are paid to manage money for their clients and aren't paid for anything else.

In my practice, by keeping our model simple, we avoid conflicts with our clients' best interests. For example, our clients like the fact that we do not charge commissions for trading like brokerage houses do. After all, if your broker gets paid a commission every time you buy or sell a stock (but not when you do not), what would you think about his recommendations to make trades?

In addition, we have few distractions from our primary mission. Because we have never been in the business of making loans or trading for our own account, we are not spending time and energy focused on our own balance sheet. We can stay focused on our clients' interests rather than our own. Our clients' interests **are** our interests.

When I first began managing money for a living, some of my clients and prospective clients would ask me if I had my own money invested at my firm. This is an excellent question to ask of a prospective advisor.

I answered that not only did I have all of my own money at my firm but that my firm managed my mother's money and my father-in-law's money.

Putting your money where your mouth is—that is one thing. Putting your father-in-law's money there—that is confidence.

Finally, one last factor you might consider when evaluating a financial advisor is that . . .

TRANSPARENCY IS ESSENTIAL.

There are no secrets to my investment strategies. I am happy to share any and all of them with you. My attention is riveted on my clients and their portfolios, and at my firm, we go to the ends of the earth to support our clients.

To conclude this chapter, I will share an anecdote that—for me at least—demonstrates the importance and difficulty of placing trust appropriately. It is a story about my youngest son, James. When James was four years old, I tried to teach him to be cautious around strangers.

James has always been a charming, friendly soul. He is a born salesman, and he loves people. This is a wonderful thing, but it makes me a bit nervous.

James and I were playing a game of Chutes and Ladders in our basement, and I asked him if he knew about strangers.

"A stranger is someone I don't know," he said.

"That's right," I said. "Are you supposed to talk to strangers?"

"No," James replied. "Only if my teacher or a policeman or someone from the family is there."

"That's right," I told him. "Let's pretend, okay?"

I told James that we were going to play a game. I told him that I was going to **pretend** to be a stranger and that he needed to show me what he should do if a stranger wanted to talk to him. James was ready to play.

I put on my scariest looking face. "Hi, little boy," I sneered. With my best Snidely Whiplash voice, I continued, "Come into my car for a moment. I have some candy for you."

James lit up with joy. "I LOVE candy!" he exclaimed.

I couldn't help but laugh. James was crestfallen. "Where is the candy?" he asked. "Is it in the car?"

As you make your way through the world of financial advisors, you may find that there are a lot of folks out there who are offering you candy. Perhaps you might not want to take all of them at their word.

By now, you are well on your way to mastering the fundamentals of financial success, which brings me to the last and most important chapter of this book. In the next chapter, you will learn what is most important to look for if you choose to hire a financial advisor. Here is a hint: it goes well beyond merely outperforming the market.

Fundamental #10:
Evaluating Your Investment Manager

The fascinating—sometimes exhilarating—work of combining imaginative research and astute portfolio management to achieve superior investment results is and has always been extraordinarily difficult.

However, difficulty is not always proportional to importance. A skilled carpenter has to master many difficult and complex skills, for example, but the simple task of properly measuring boards before he begins a project is one of the most important parts of his job. Similarly, although it surprises many laypeople, studies have consistently shown that the most important determinant of success in a medical procedure isn't the surgical team's talent; it is the cleanliness of the operating room.

What is most difficult is not necessarily most important. Sometimes simple things matter the most.

Likewise, the most valuable part of what investment professionals do—namely, investment planning and counseling—can often seem like the least difficult part of the job.

Investment research and portfolio management requires specialized expertise and complex financial models. Investment planning and counseling can seem simpler than investment research and portfolio management, but I believe that effective planning is one of the most important determinants of financial success.

Effective investment counseling takes time and hard work. Effective investment advice should be based on knowledge of diverse and complex markets. Most importantly, good advice is predicated on knowledge of diverse and complex people: clients.

Successful investment counselors help each client understand how the risks of investing apply to that client's unique financial life. Good financial advisors work alongside their clients to set realistic investment objectives and plan to achieve those objectives through realistic spending and saving goals. Successful advisors help clients understand the tradeoffs among appropriate asset classes. Those advisors build resilient portfolios and help clients avoid overreactions to market highs or lows.

In Chapters 8 and 9, I suggested that investors should seek out advisors who will prioritize their clients' best interests. The best advice I can give you in selecting an investment advisor is to:

- Find someone who will listen.

- Don't confuse luck with skill.

- Understand that good investors are modest investors.
- Focus on measures that reflect performance over the long term.
- Separate and evaluate both alpha and asset allocation when comparing investment managers.

The first thing you might consider in hiring an investment advisor is . . .

FIND SOMEONE WHO WILL LISTEN.

That is, you should find someone who will listen to you describe your unique goals and circumstances. You should find someone who will assist you in translating your hopes and fears into a meaningful, practical financial plan. Someone who will treat your plan as a living document, working with you and your other professional advisors to adjust course as things change. Someone who will keep you informed of what is happening with your investments and, most importantly, will always stay informed of what is happening in your financial life. Someone whose investment strategies change with your changing circumstances as well as with changes in the markets.

Most people who interview prospective financial advisors start and end their questions with a narrow view of performance. They want to see how each product the advisor recommends—stocks, bonds, real estate, etc.—performed over the last one, three, or five years against a set of benchmarks and/or peer comparisons.

As discussed earlier in this book, being able to outperform a benchmark or a peer group (i.e., generating alpha) is important. It is a necessary but insufficient part of what a good investment manager does.

In fact, generating alpha is much less important than most investors assume it is. The most important thing your investment advisor does is provide sound advice—good counsel in difficult times—and a plan that is flexible enough to accommodate the inevitable changes that occur in the markets and the changes that will occur in your own financial life.

Investors who work with managers who generate alpha but do not provide good investment counsel ultimately can do quite poorly; they can end up with much less wealth over time than will people who have the benefit of working with a true professional planner.

Nonetheless, investors focus on alpha, and they should—just not to the exclusion of everything else. In focusing on alpha, investors should not just focus on how **much** alpha an investment manager creates; they should also focus on exactly **how** that alpha is created.

The way investment results are achieved is at least as important as the investment results themselves. After all, there are hundreds of thousands of people who hold themselves out as investment managers. Statistically, exactly 50% will be better than average. Even if every investment manager limited his investment approach to just throwing darts at a dartboard, the law of large numbers guarantees that some will have phenomenal investment records.

It is important to acknowledge that . . .

LUCK AND SKILL ARE NOT THE SAME.

In practice, it can be hard to tell the difference. Confusing one for the other can be costly.

Investors can be right for the wrong reasons or wrong for the right reasons. In hindsight, most people only see the outcomes of—not the inputs to—the investment model that leads to a given investment. So, if an investor who buys a stock because he expects a certain outcome is entirely wrong about his investment thesis, but for completely unrelated reasons, the stock goes up, that investor appears to be a genius (and invariably accepts the credit that comes his way).

Another investor may correctly divine that a company's future earnings will be greater than anticipated and buy that company's stock but is penalized when the market sells off the stock for unrelated reasons. This investor may make excuses, but he will likely be judged by his returns rather than his research.

Imagine that every day, every one of 300 million Americans flip a dollar coin and predicts whether the coin will end up heads or tails. Those who are right get a dollar and are allowed to compete again the next day, wagering all the money they won the prior day against that day's outcome.

After ten days, almost 300,000 people will have called their coin flips correctly and won $1,000. They may try to be modest about this, but some people will certainly take note of the winners' ability to toss coins and predict the outcome of those tosses. After another ten days, there will still be more than 200 people who have called their coins correctly 20 times in a row, and they will have each been rewarded with more than $1 million apiece for their efforts. Perhaps not all 200 will be writing books with titles like *How to Make a Million Dollars in Just Minutes a Day* or speaking to groups of people who want to follow their approach to making money, but some of them will.

Investing and gambling aren't the same thing, but gambling can look like investing if you don't look closely. Many of the investment professionals who write books or host TV shows followed paths that required just as much luck and just as much skill as the coin-flippers described above.

Whether a decision is correct or incorrect cannot be judged based on the outcome of the decision. This is true in investing and in many other aspects of life. Driving drunk is always a bad decision—regardless of whether you are lucky enough to avoid an accident. Investing based on a hunch or a gut feeling is always a bad decision—regardless of whether you are lucky enough to make money. A good decision is an optimal decision given all the facts that are knowable when the decision is made—not given all the facts that are knowable after the outcomes are clear. Correct decisions can lead to unsuccessful outcomes and vice versa.

Good investors—and good investment professionals— understand they cannot fully predict or avoid the forces of fate. As such, . . .

GOOD INVESTORS ARE MODEST INVESTORS.

When asked about the future, good investors always answer "I don't know," "I can't be sure," or "Here is what is more or less probable."

I am most comfortable with investors who have a reliable research-based approach to the markets. I look for and respect investors who utilize a rigorous system of reviewing and ranking different investment opportunities and apply those tools with consistency over time.

It is always the case that past performance is no guarantee of future results. If you look carefully at the tiny print that accompanies most of the marketing investment companies produce, you will often see those words. Those warnings are certainly true when the process that guided past performance differs from the process guiding future results or when there is no real process for investment decisions at all.

Process is important to investment performance and so are the people responsible for that investment performance.

You should be wary of companies that use a "star system."[63] Research analysts come and go. People retire, seek greener pastures, get hit by buses (both proverbially and literally). Investment managers who use the star system can fall apart if just one person leaves the company, so make sure your investment manager has a deep bench to draw on if changes occur.

Fundamental #10

Finally, as you are evaluating performance in the narrowest terms of alpha, be sure to . . .

LOOK AT MEASURES THAT REFLECT PERFORMANCE OVER THE LONG TERM.

Please do not chase short-term performance. Investors who focus on short-term performance nearly always end up undermining their long-term ability to create and preserve wealth.[64]

As a reminder of this, you might refer back to the chart on page 71 in Chapter 6, which shows how much the average investor underperforms the benchmark index. I have studied this underperformance extensively over the years, and I have learned a lot about what drives these sorts of gaps. It is not so much that investors choose bad funds; it is that they tend to sell what has recently performed poorly and buy whatever is hot at the moment. Investors end up buying high and selling low with the exact opposite results of what they hope for.

My role as a financial advisor is to help clients avoid the common mistakes that emotional human beings are prone to make. I do this by providing my clients with information and an investment platform that encourages more productive long-term investing.

If alpha is interesting, then asset allocation is critical, as we discussed at length in Chapter 6. To illustrate this point I looked at my firm's own data and experience with clients over the past 30 years. I compared our clients' performance as attributable to our asset-allocation choices (i.e., the results sourced by choosing asset mixes in our various fully diversified constructions) versus the results achieved by the average U.S. household as computed by the Federal Reserve. I found that since 1983, our clients added 1.8 percentage points of return each year (compounded) simply by following our asset-allocation advice.

If you had 10% in international stocks and your manager produced alpha, and I had 30% in international stocks and did not produce alpha, who won? Well, international stocks significantly outperformed U.S. equities over the past five years, so my portfolio – with more international stocks—would almost certainly outperform yours (with fewer but better performing international stocks).

Thus, when comparing managers . . .

YOU NEED TO SEPARATE AND EVALUATE BOTH ALPHA AND ASSET ALLOCATION.

By reviewing both asset-class performance and asset-allocation advice, you can properly understand and evaluate performance. Ultimately, the alpha posted by top-quartile managers is dwarfed by the contribution a good manager can make through rebalancing, asset allocation (dynamic and otherwise), tax management, and wealth planning—not every year but over time.

***

This chapter—and much of this book—has focused on choosing and evaluating advisors who can assist you with your financial planning and in building and monitoring your investment portfolios.

It is worth noting that your financial advisor cannot do his best work for you on his own. Your financial advisor should work closely with the bankers, accountants, lawyers, and other professionals who also have your best interests at heart. Finding the right team of professionals to support you is an important part of building and protecting your financial success.

How should you start your planning process—or take the next step in your financial journey? You might begin by seeking out one professional—an investment advisor, banker, lawyer, or accountant—who can act as the quarterback or "team captain" for the team of professionals you will build together.

As I mentioned in Chapter 5, you might ask your friends or colleagues for advice. Do they have an estate planning attorney whom they trust? An accountant they really like? An advisor who has done great work for them? You might begin by interviewing these professionals. You might ask them how they work with clients like you. And when you find someone whom you like and trust and respect—perhaps an accountant, perhaps a financial advisor, perhaps a banker or a lawyer—ask them to tell you whom else they respect in the professional community.

Planning is a team sport. Your investment advisor is an important part of your financial team – but not the only part.

Every lesson that I have suggested in this book has been enhanced and improved by the many fine accountants, lawyers, bankers, and other professionals with whom I have worked over the years. None of us are as good alone as all of us are together.

Epilogue

Now that we have gone through the ten fundamentals of financial success, I would like to leave you with one last lesson that has always served me well . . .

FAILURE TEACHES MORE THAN SUCCESS.

Conan O'Brien made this point perfectly in his speech to the Harvard Class of 2000. He was speaking about his first late night talk show:

> *We debuted on September 13, 1993, and I was really happy, really happy, with our effort. I felt like I had seized the moment, that I had put my very best foot forward.*
>
> *And this was what the most respected and widely read television critic, Tom Shales, wrote in The Washington Post. "O'Brien is a living collage of annoying nervous habits.*

He giggles and jiggles about and fiddles with his cuffs. He has dark, beady little eyes like a rabbit. He is one of the whitest white men ever. O'Brien is a switch on the guest who won't leave: he's the host who should never have come. Let the Late Show with Conan O'Brien become the late Late Show, and may the host return to whence he came." There's more, but it gets kind of mean.

. . . I took a lot of criticism, some of it deserved, some of it excessive, and, to be honest with you, it hurt like you would not believe. But I'm telling you all this for a reason. I've had a lot of success. I've had a lot of failure. I've looked good. I've looked bad. I've been praised. And I've been criticized. But my mistakes have been necessary. I've dwelled on my failures today because . . . your biggest liability is your need to succeed, your need to always find yourself on the sweet side of the bell curve. Success is a lot like a bright white tuxedo. You feel terrific when you get it, but then you're desperately afraid of getting it dirty, of spoiling it.

. . . [E]very failure was freeing, and today I'm as nostalgic for the bad as I am for the good. So that's what I wish for all of you—the bad as well as the good. Fall down. Make a mess. Break something occasionally. Know that your mistakes are your own unique way of getting to where you need to be. And remember that the story is never over.

. . . If you can laugh at yourself, loud and hard, every time you fall, people will think you're drunk. Thank you.[65]

I hope you can find comfort in Conan's advice as you continue your financial journey. Just as in life, there are ups and downs to investing, and there are going to be times when your plan simply doesn't go the way you want it to go. As Woody Allen has been credited with saying, "If you want to make God laugh, tell Him your plans."

I would simply say this: a little laughter . . . and a lot of planning… can be a good thing.

Pulling everything together from throughout this book, here are the main lessons you might take away from our time together:

- Markets—and many investors—are rarely rational in the short term. Over the long term, a rational investor can profit from markets that are irrational in the short term. Maintaining rationality in the face of irrational markets is harder than it might seem.

- Investing based on (your own) fear and greed is the definition of irrational investing. It is likely to be comforting in the short term but to be damaging to your wealth over time.

- One way to become wealthy is to work hard doing something you enjoy, something that you are good at, and something that provides significant financial rewards for success. This is not the only way to become wealthy, but it is a pretty good approach.

- An investment manager who tells you he can make you wealthy is lying to you, lying to himself, or both. Becoming wealthy is your job. Your investment manager's job is not to make you wealthy; it is to help preserve, protect, and grow your wealth over time. Preserving and protecting your wealth starts with spending less than you earn, and to do that consistently over time, you need a good financial plan.

- Risk in an investment portfolio should be considered from the perspective of the portfolio as a whole—not by looking at the performance of any asset on its own. Two very volatile assets may be risky to hold on their own but have little risk if held together (depending on the correlation between their returns).

- An asset that seems safe—like cash, gold, or Treasuries— can have real risks if, for example, inflation rises and erodes your purchasing power or the asset's price has already been bid up in the marketplace.

- The fact that an asset has appreciated in price recently does not make it safer, and the fact that an asset has depreciated in price recently does not make it riskier.

- A good financial plan is multigenerational.

- Financial plans are living documents, and your plans are out of date as soon as your financial circumstances change. Keep your plan updated. Providing your financial planner with updated information on your financial circumstances is your job. Updating the plan and keeping you informed of the consequences is your advisor's job.

- Taxes matter. Income taxes, capital gains taxes, gift taxes, and estate taxes. They all matter. Money that you pay in taxes is money that does not go to your family or charities.

- Just because something is cheap, doesn't mean it is a good value. Just because something is expensive, doesn't mean it is overpriced.

- A diversified investment portfolio includes assets that perform in different ways at different points in time. Diversification is not just about adding more or different things to a portfolio. Too much of "more" or "different" just adds cost and complexity. If you do not understand the diversification benefit of a given investment, do not add it to your portfolio.

- Assessing value—the difference between the current price of an asset and the value of the future income stream that asset can produce—is the most reliable way to invest over time.

- Many people who offer financial advice are unqualified to do so, and many have interests that are not aligned with yours.

- The most important service your investment advisor provides to you is the financial plan you craft together. The next most important service your investment advisor provides is his ability to maintain and adjust your plan as markets and circumstances change.

- Most investment professionals overestimate their ability to outperform a benchmark over time.

- Most investors overestimate their ability to choose an investment professional who can outperform a benchmark over time.

- Most investors overestimate the importance of outperforming a benchmark over time.

- It is easy—and expensive—to confuse luck with skill in investing.

I hope you will find the time and the inclination to begin the planning process early, update your financial plans as often as your circumstances change, and involve and encourage a team of trusted professionals to assist you throughout this process. If you do all this, I believe you will find that planning provides a sure and true path to real investment success and peace of mind.

Words of Wisdom[66]

Don't put all of your eggs in one basket. Don't put your eggs in too many baskets. Choose the right baskets, and then watch those baskets carefully.

Without data, there are no facts—only opinions.

You are welcome to your own opinions—just not your own facts.

What counts most is often most difficult to count.

If it sounds too good to be true, it probably is.

Don't confuse activity with accomplishment.

Don't confuse wisdom with a bull market.

Markets are rational in the long term but not in the short term. If you don't mind being rational and wrong in the short term, you can make money over time. Being irrational and right in the short term is a good way to lose everything over time.

Markets can stay irrational longer than you can stay liquid.

In the long run, we're all dead.

Bubbles eventually burst.

Investing minus time equals gambling.[67]

It's tough to make predictions, especially about the future.

Everyone has a plan until they get punched in the face.

Money won't buy happiness, but it will pay the salaries of a large research staff to study the problem.

You will do better by investing with a lousy manager in a great market than you will with a great manager in a lousy market.

Eventually the impossible becomes inevitable.

You make most of your money in a bear market. You just don't realize it at the time.

Good times teach bad lessons.

Everything should be made as simple as possible and no simpler.

A pessimist believes that things can't possibly get any worse. An optimist believes that they can.

There are two kinds of economists—those who can't predict the future and those who don't know that they can't predict the future.

There are two kinds of investors who lose money—those who know everything and those who know nothing.

The richest man is the man who owns the most of his own time.

No man is rich enough to buy back his own past.

Common sense isn't always common practice.

Economic forecasters exist to make astrologers look good.

If you don't know who you are, the stock market is an expensive place to find out.

About the Author

David Greene is a vice president and financial advisor with the Washington, DC, office of Bernstein Global Wealth Management. He advises high-net-worth individuals and institutions regarding investment strategies and, in conjunction with Bernstein's Wealth Management Group, works closely with clients and their professional advisors on a wide range of investment matters, including tax and estate planning, concentrated stock positions, and the sale of privately held businesses.

Prior to joining AllianceBernstein, Mr. Greene spent seven years at The Washington Post Company, where he served as the president of PostNewsweek Tech Media. Mr. Greene came to The Washington Post Company from the Atlanta office of McKinsey & Company, a global management consulting firm.

Mr. Greene graduated *magna cum laude* with a degree in economics from Harvard College, where he was elected to *Phi Beta Kappa*. Mr. Greene received his MBA with honors from Harvard Business School.

Mr. Greene and his wife Gayle currently reside in Vienna, Virginia, with their children Robert, James, and Elizabeth.

Endnotes

1. This story of Charles Mackay was—to the best of my knowledge—originally reported by Andrew Odlyzko and was recounted by Jason Zweig in his excellent column in *The Wall Street Journal*, *"The Intelligent Investor."* Zweig, J. (2011, November 5). Why spotting bubbles is harder than it looks. *The Wall Street Journal*. Retrieved from http://online.wsj.com/article/SB10001424052970204621904577017960729384948.html.

2. As far as I know, Mean Joe Greene is not related to me, Not-So-Mean David Greene.

3. Freeland, C. (2011, January-February). The rise of the new global elite. *The Atlantic*. Retrieved from http://www.theatlantic.com/magazine/archive/2011/01/the-rise-of-the-new-global-elite/308343/.

4. A note on the footnotes: The first time I remember footnotes being interesting was in Dave Eggers' book, A Heartbreaking Work of Staggering Genius. I think Eggers was inspired by David Foster Wallace and Nicholson Baker (among others), so I attribute him with inspiring me but not with originality—at least not in this instance. Of course, I claim no originality on my part—probably woefully little inspiration as well, heartbreaking and staggering as that may be.

5. Jobs, S. (2005, June). Commencement Address. Speech delivered to Stanford University, Palo Alto, CA. Retrieved from http://news.stanford.edu/news/2005/june15/jobs-061505.html.

6. Readers of an early draft of this book suggested that additional worthwhile material on this topic can be found in Marsha Sinetar's

1989 book, *Do What You Love, The Money Will Follow: Discovering Your Right Livelihood*.

7. Dorothy Parker figured this out before I did and said it better.

8. I never worked at Ti-D Toilet (a fictional company, as far as I know), nor have I worked at any other fictional or non-fictional toilet-related manufacturing company. No offense intended to the many fine fictional and non-fictional men and women who do or did.

9. It turns out that—at least as of this writing—*Good Housekeeping* still exists in magazine form. When I had this conversation in 1996, everyone knew the magazine and its research institute. The Good Housekeeping Seal of Approval has been around for more than 100 years, but I wonder if it will be around for the next 100 years. Probably not, at least not as currently constituted.

10. Gardner, J. (1990, November). Personal Renewal. Speech delivered to McKinsey & Company in Phoenix, AZ. Retrieved from http://www.pbs.org/johngardner/sections/writings_speech_1.html.

11. Ibarra, H. (2002, December). How to stay stuck in the wrong career. *Harvard Business Review.* Retrieved from http://hbr.org/product/how-to-stay-stuck-in-the-wrong-career/an/R0212B-PDF-ENG.

12. Readers of an early draft of this book recommended additional related exercises, which can be found in Richard Bolles' What Color Is Your Parachute?

13. Barry Schwartz, a professor of social theory at Swarthmore College. Quoted in Gottlieb, L. (2011 July-August). How to land your kid in therapy. *The Atlantic.* Retrieved from http://www.theatlantic.com/magazine/archive/2011/07/how-to-land-your-kid-in-therapy/308555/

14. I am afraid this might have been the trap that caught me had I gone to work for Ti-D Toilet. Not that Ti-D Toilet isn't a great company—it is. Or, it would be if it actually existed. However, if it existed, it probably wouldn't have been right for me.

15. Throughout this book, I have illustrated examples using a 60/40 portfolio—a portfolio that is composed of 60% globally diversified stocks and 40% intermediate-duration bonds. Although a 60/40 portfolio is a very common model portfolio used in financial analysis and illustrations, it is not the right portfolio for every client in every situation. The asset allocation of your accounts should be customized to your unique circumstances. In determining the asset allocation that

any given client should use in any given account, I give consideration to factors that include the unique goals of the client and the need for growth in the account, the time horizon of the money and the need for principal protection in the account over shorter periods of time, and the tax characteristics of the account and the tax situation of the client.

16. Even if he should live longer than expected, suffer higher inflation than expected, and see abysmal investment returns.

17. These spending rates are for couples and assume an allocation of 60% globally diversified stocks (70% U.S., 25% developed foreign markets, 5% emerging markets) and 40% diversified intermediate-term municipal bonds. Spending is a percentage of the initial value of the portfolio and is grown with inflation. Spending rates assume maintaining spending with a 95% level of confidence based on estimates of the range of returns for the applicable capital markets over the periods analyzed.

    All information on longevity and mortality-adjusted investment analysis is based on mortality tables compiled in 2000. In our mortality analysis, the lifespan of an individual varies in each of our 10,000 trials in accordance with mortality tables.

    Society of Actuaries RP-2000 mortality tables and AllianceBernstein.

18. Ghilarducci, T. (2012 July 21). Our ridiculous approach to retirement. *The New York Times*. Retrieve from http://www.nytimes.com/2012/07/22/opinion/sunday/our-ridiculous-approach-to-retirement.html

19. Well done, by the way.

20. Outperforming the market by 1% is indeed really hard. Most active managers do not outperform the market over time. And, over recent years, very few active managers have outperformed the market. It is easy to see why many investors have made the decision to use passive investment approaches like index funds. However, index funds and other passive investment approaches have their own challenges and risks.

    I am not advocating passive investing. Indeed, my firm invests hundreds of millions of dollars each year in research designed to help our clients actively outperform the markets.

    I am simply suggesting that finding an active investment manager who outperforms the markets will not solve a spending problem.

21. Presumably, you are not yourself a financial advisor who gets to talk about money—what it buys and what it cannot buy, how people think about it, how it changes people—with your clients. If you were, then you probably would not be reading my book. The next best thing to talking with people about money and what it can and can't do may be the academic research in the field of consumer consumption and happiness (in particular, you might look toward the work of Elizabeth Dunn, Daniel Gilbert, and Timothy Wilson).

22. To recap, this book is not an advice manual on saving and spending money, and it is not a book of career advice. I have failed in this book to provide my readers with any get-rich-quick schemes. In addition, this is not a book that provides advice on different comparative approaches to investing (e.g., selecting individual stocks/bonds on your own versus buying mutual funds versus working with a discretionary money manager). This is not a book that details different investment approaches or financial terms (e.g., top-down versus bottom-up investing or sell-side versus buy-side investment management). This book simply describes what I have learned from building and managing financial plans with my clients. This book is designed for investors who want to work with a financial planner and want to understand how to find the best financial advisor for their particular needs. I have tried to describe in detail what clients should ask of their advisors, how clients might work with their advisors, and how clients can evaluate their advisors and the plans they create with them.

23. I have a client who tends to be somewhat right-of-center in his politics. He tells me that he starts each day by reading *The Post* and *The Times*. "*The New York Post* and *The Washington Times*," he is quick to add.

24. Dunn, E., and Norton, M. (2012, July 7). Don't indulge. Be happy. *The New York Times*. Retrieved from http://www.nytimes.com/2012/07/08/opinion/sunday/dont-indulge-be-happy.html?pagewanted=all.

25. For one overview, see Clark, A., Frijters, P., and Shields, M. (2008). Relative income, happiness, and utility: An explanation for the Easterlin Paradox and other puzzles. *Journal of Economic Literature, 46(1), 95–144.*

26. As Yogi Berra (among others) is said to have said, "It's tough to make predictions, especially about the future." This is so wise that I have included it twice in this book—here and in the "Words of Wisdom" section.

27. As Donald Rumsfeld said, "There are known knowns. These are things

we know that we know. There are known unknowns. That is to say, there are things that we know we don't know. But there are also unknown unknowns. There are things we don't know we don't know." All these things—the known knowns, the known unknowns, and the unknown unknowns—change over time. Good planning incorporates them all.

28. Names have been changed to protect the innocent. Sadly, most investment professionals don't do anything to protect the innocent. Caveat emptor.

29. Again, I am not promoting indexing as the right investment solution for everyone or suggesting that good active managers cannot outperform passive investment strategies over time. I am simply suggesting that if you are going to hire an active manager and pay the fees and costs associated with active management, then you should get all the benefits of the active management for which you are paying. You cannot get those benefits if you hire a manager who hugs the benchmark. You cannot reap those benefits if you hire multiple active managers who are not coordinating their investment decisions across their varied and various portfolios. If you want the benefit of active management, then you need to hire a single active manager (at the very least, for every given asset class if not for your entire portfolio).

One of the challenges of indexing, since we are on the topic, is that indexes can become distorted as different stocks or sectors outperform. For example, in 1980, as energy stocks became more expensive, they became a larger and larger part of the S&P 500 index. Ultimately, energy stocks made up a 27% share of the S&P 500 in 1980 (and then declined in value by 51.1% over the next two years). By 1999, technology stocks had grown to be the largest component of the S&P 500—and then led the market down over the next two years, declining by more than 56%. Financials played a similar role in 2006, becoming the largest portion of the S&P 500 Index and then declining by nearly 64% in the two years that followed. Active managers adjust their investments in response to these distortions.

30. Barclays Capital; Compustat; Moody's Investors Service; Standard & Poor's; U.S. Bureau of Labor Statistics; AllianceBernstein; Ibbotson, R. G. and Sinquefield, R. A. (1976, January). Stocks, bonds, bills, and inflation: Year-by-year historical returns. *The Journal of Business*.

31. Based on a simulation of after-tax returns (assuming 2012 tax rates that include a 15% long-term capital gains rate and a 35% short-term rate) over nearly three decades.

32. Occasionally (as has happened in recent years), we have also done the reverse, buying municipal bonds in tax-free bond accounts when municipal yields have been higher than taxable yields on a risk-adjusted basis.

33. It is made more complex by the fact that Congress continuously changes the tax laws in ways that may affect taxable accounts, tax-deferred accounts, and the dynamics of allocating assets between and holding assets in both categories of accounts.

34. No one will ever admit this, of course. Go ahead and ask a broker whether his firm manages taxes efficiently and effectively in his clients' accounts. Then ask him exactly how his firm does this. Then watch him squirm.

35. Inflation measured by the US Consumer Price Index (CPI), US City Average, all items, not seasonally adjusted.

36. Stocks represented by the S&P 500 (with a Global Financial Data extension) and bonds by 10-year US Treasuries.

37. For an excellent overview of the topic of protecting clients against the risks of inflation, please see "Deflating Inflation: Redefining the Inflation-Resistant Portfolio" AllianceBernstein (March 2010).

38. One good reason to use multiple investment managers is expertise. You might choose one manager who is exceptionally good at understanding and investing in U.S. large-cap companies, another who is very good at understanding the municipal bond market, and so on. However, using multiple managers comes with certain costs: the difficulty of rebalancing your investments across multiple managers, greater fees and complexity, etc. Hiring multiple managers to manage the same kinds of investments (e.g., having two managers, each of whom is tasked with investing in emerging market stocks) creates even more challenges, especially when it comes to managing taxes and maintaining an appropriate level of diversification and risk control within that single asset class.

39. Andrew Carnegie figured this out before I did and said it better.

40. Real Estate Investment Trusts (REITs) are represented by the National Association of Real Estate Investment Trusts (NAREIT) Index, bonds by the Lehman Brothers Aggregate Bond Index, U.S. value stocks by the Russell 1000 Value Index, international stocks by the Morgan Stanley Capital International (MSCI) Europe, Australia, and Far East (EAFE) Index with countries weighted by market capitalization and

currencies un-hedged, U.S. growth stocks by the Russell 1000 Growth Index, and emerging markets stocks by the IFC World Bank Global Index for 1987 and the MSCI Emerging Markets Index thereafter.

IFC, Lehman Brothers, MSCI, NAREIT, Russell Investment Group, and AllianceBernstein.

41. U.S. returns are represented by the S&P 500; all other country returns are represented by MSCI local indexes. Source: MSCI, Standard & Poor's, and AllianceBernstein.

42. Cash plays an important part in every investor's life, and most investors would benefit from a strong relationship with a banker who can help with cash management. However, as a diversifier to stocks in an investment portfolio, cash is a poor substitute for bonds.

43. S&P 500 returns: Standard & Poor's.

44. Lipper Municipal Bond Index Blend: a combination of the Lipper Short Municipal, Lipper Short-Intermediate Municipal, and Lipper Intermediate Municipal.

45. S&P 500 returns: Standard & Poor's.

46. Lipper Municipal Bond Index Blend: a combination of the Lipper Short Municipal, Lipper Short-Intermediate Municipal, and Lipper Intermediate Municipal.

47. Fund flows through December 31, 2011, represented by total net new cash into U.S. equity funds. Investment Company Institute, Standard & Poor's, Strategic Insight, and AllianceBernstein.

48. Dalbar, Inc. *2010 QAIB Quantitative Analysis of Investor Behavior.*

49. Actual wealth results are based on simulations using historical index returns. Both investors start with a 60% equity/40% bond allocation, but the performance chaser raises and lowers his equity allocation near market peaks and troughs, while the rebalancer maintains a 60%/40% allocation. Barclays Capital, Lipper, MSCI, Russell Investment Group, U.S. Bureau of Labor Statistics, and AllianceBernstein.

50. Based on the ranking of money managers by asset classes as reported by Informa Investment Solutions (PSN). The first quartile of managers' performance for value, growth, international, and intermediate municipal bonds are averaged over all rolling 10-year periods beginning January 1,

1983, to December 31, 2010. Emerging markets are added beginning January 1, 1988.

The average for each asset class is then weighted to calculate the overall performance of a 60% stock/40% bond account.

The weighting is set at 21% value, 21% growth, 15% international, 3% emerging markets, and 40% municipal bonds. We then assume a fee of 1% to arrive at the after-fee added value of hiring the top quartile manager in each asset class.

Barclays Capital, MSCI, Standard & Poor's, and Alliance Bernstein.

51. By the way, this is exceptionally difficult to do. If you are choosing one manager in one asset class, you have a one-out-of-four chance of choosing a top-quartile manager (i.e., a manager in the top 25% of all managers). If you are choosing managers in two asset classes, you have a one-out-of-sixteen chance of having both managers be in the top 25% of their respective universes (.25% times .25%). If you are choosing managers in five asset classes, you have less than a one-out-of-one-thousand chance of choosing all five in the top quartile (.25% times .25% times .25% times .25% times .25% = 1 out of 1,024).

52. From 1991 through 2010, the S&P 500 returned 9.1% per year, and the Barclays Aggregate Bond Index returned 6.9% per year. Of course, this 20-year period includes one of the longest and most dramatic bond rallies in history and two significant stock market bubbles and crashes.

53. S&P 500 versus Lipper Municipal Bond Index.

54. And, as discussed in Chapter 5, because no one can reliably predict how any given asset class will perform in any given period, diversifying is also important.

55. As discussed in Chapter 4, costs matter. Taxes matter. A good investment plan and a good investment planner takes costs and taxes into account.

56. Return premium from rebalancing a 50/50 growth and value portfolio 1978–2011, assuming quarterly rebalancing from 1978 through 1982 and monthly rebalancing thereafter.

57. Purchasing power is the amount of goods and services that a unit of value can buy. Some investors claim (for example) that the price of an ounce of gold has roughly equaled the cost of a good men's suit over time. If that were the case, then gold would have maintained its purchasing power

over time. An asset that is increasing in value in real terms would be increasing its purchasing power over time.

58. Nominal rates have not been adjusted for inflation. For example, if Treasuries are paying a 5% interest rate and inflation is running at 3%, then the nominal yield on Treasuries is 5%, but the inflation-adjusted rate (also called the real rate) is 2% (5%–3%).

59. Data on gold and Treasuries taken from "What's Safe?" AllianceBernstein, October 2011.

60. Calculations for core capital and actual results are based on an allocation of 60% global stocks and 40% intermediate-duration municipal bonds. Global Financial Data; Moody's Investors Service; Standard & Poor's; U.S. Bureau of Labor Statistics; AllianceBernstein; Ibbotson, R. G. and Sinquefield, R. A. (1976, January). Stocks, bonds, bills, and inflation: Year-by-year historical returns. *The Journal of Business*.

61. Ibid.

62. As the author of an investment book, I recognize and appreciate the irony of this statement.

63. A reader of an early draft of this book thought this reference was a criticism of Morningstar, which is known for their "star system." In fact, what I am referencing here is my concern for investors who put their faith in "superstar" managers—firms who hire well-known individuals with powerful track records. I have more faith in managers who work in teams. Managers who work in teams are more likely to have a rigorous and replicable investment approach, and they are less likely to get hit by buses (at least, it is less likely that all the members of the team will all get hit by buses at the same time). No comment on Morningstar or its rating system was intended.

64. Please recall the difference in results between the rebalancer and the performance chaser in Chapter 6.

65. O'Brien, C. (2000, June). Commencement Address. Speech delivered to Harvard University, Cambridge, MA. Retrieved from http://www.allowe.com/Humor/book/COBspeech2k.htm.

66. Many colleagues, clients, and confidants have provided these words of wisdom to me over the years. Some (e.g., "Don't confuse wisdom with a bull market") seem impossible to source. Surely, someone must have put this idea to paper first, but it became part of conventional wisdom

so long ago that the author seems to be lost to history. Other aphorisms have disputed sources. I've been told that both Samuel Goldwyn and Yogi Berra were the originator of "It's tough to make predictions, especially about the future." I am fairly certain that Mike Tyson is the source of the quote "Everyone has a plan until they get punched in the face," which is a particular favorite of mine.

67. This happens to be one of my favorite sayings despite the fact that it seems to confuse a lot of people. It may be true that if you have to explain a joke, there is no joke. However, I like to think that an explanation can be justified (and helpful) when it comes to financial aphorisms.

So, here is the idea behind this saying. "Investing minus time equals gambling" is how I respond to people who come up to me at cocktail parties and say, "I have some money to invest, but I need the money back at the end of the year. Where should I invest?"

I like to respond, "Investing minus time equals gambling." In other words, if you need the money back within a year, then putting that money into stocks or gold or any other volatile asset today is not investing. It is gambling. You may have better odds in the stock market or the commodities market than you would find at a casino. However, over short periods of time, there is no such thing as investing. There is saving, and there is gambling. Investing takes time.